Daily Habits of
Intimacy with God

Published by Tulsa Therapy for Women. Tulsa, Oklahoma.

ISBN: 978-0-578-15234-9

For more information: http://www.tulsatherapyforwomen.com

Cover provided by Cameron Ann Coblentz

Some of the anecdotal illustrations in this book are true to life and are included with the permission of persons involved. All other illustrations are composites of real situations, and any resemblance to people living or dead is coincidence.

* * *

About Roselene Coblentz

Roselene Coblentz is a marriage and family therapist in Tulsa, Oklahoma. She is committed to serving others through prayer, teaching, counseling, mentoring, and now writing.

Roselene and her husband Lloyd of 35 years live in Broken Arrow, Oklahoma.

Roselene is a woman who sits with Jesus and lives a real life transformed by His perfect love. She spends significant time in God's Word and in prayer, and she lives her days to be one with Jesus. God's healing love has flowed into my life through her grace filled way of living and sharing truth. My life and the lives of my family are forever changed because of God's work through her. Everyone who experiences Roselene experiences the beauty of God's healing, freedom, and light.

Lindsey Morris

Roselene is not only my mother, but I am also privileged to call her my close friend. Throughout the years she has always been my cheerleader and her words and actions have taught me to seek God and pursue Him with my whole heart. Even in my darkest moments, my mother has been there to love, counsel, and most of all, pray for me. She has been an excellent role model for me in spending time with God, reading His Word, journaling my prayers, and being committed to trusting and obeying God with my life. Her life goal and passion have always been to help others know Him and experience His healing in their lives. I truly pray that the words contained in these pages are as much of an inspiration to others as they have been to me.

Cameron Coblentz

Have you ever met anyone that loves intimacy with God, family, and friends? I have. It is my friend Roselene. Have you ever met anyone that loves you unconditionally, warts and all? I have. It is my friend Roselene. Have you ever met anyone that celebrates your successes, helps you recover from your failures, and encourages you to live fully "in the ordinary?" I have. It is my friend Roselene. Have you ever met anyone that lives what they teach and believe and challenges you to do the same? I have. It is my friend Roselene. All her qualities remind me of Jesus, and after spending time with her, there are times I'm not sure who I've been with...Him or Roselene. They are so much the same.

Nancy O'Neal

Roselene's life is a reflection of "I can do all things through Christ who gives me strength." She has kept her eyes fixed on Jesus and has allowed God to mold her into the amazing Christlike woman she is today! Roselene has incredible Biblical knowledge in both mind and heart. She is a gifted counselor, teacher, speaker, and writer. I'm so blessed to call her my forever friend and am excited to see where God leads her next!

Linda Anderson

Roselene has been my friend for over 30 years. Time and distance have separated us much of the time, but whenever we get together, I am encouraged by the incredible work God is doing in her life. Through much prayer, time in God's Word, counseling, and support from other believers, Roselene has received healing for her heart and life. She has continued to move forward: growing in confidence and courage, understanding grace and forgiveness, and recognizing the role of the Holy Spirit to love and help others with their pain. She's a beautiful example of a woman who lives a God-centered life. I am blessed to know her and call her my friend!

Cheryl Direnfeld

For more information regarding the ministry and practice of Dr. Roselene Coblentz, please visit http://www.tulsatherapyforwomen.com.

Dedication

I dedicate this teaching manual to God. As the Word says, "But by the grace of God I am what I am" (1 Corinthians 15:10, NIV). All is God, All is Good, and All is Grace! This is all Him. May it declare His grace, glory, and goodness to every person who takes this intimacy journey.

I dedicate this also to my daughter, Cameron Ann, who is my legacy to know God, to be known by Him, and to love and serve others from a servant's heart. May you journey well!

Acknowledgements

Expressing gratitude is an amazing gift to offer others. My life journey includes so many, but I want to focus on those who have made *Daily Habits of Intimacy with God* a reality. First, I want to express gratefulness to Gary and Linda Dangerfield. They played a significant role in my life. At age 16, a very difficult time in my life, Gary shared the gospel message with me. The Holy Spirit brought understanding to my life, and I chose to accept God's invitation to begin a relationship with Him. I am indebted to Dr. William Backus who journeyed with me for two years, resetting a foundation of truth in my life. I trust I will be honorable to his legacy in helping others discover truth in their lives. I give thanks to Eddie and Kathy, pastors of the church I attended who were gracious counselors to me. Graphic designer Joe Carson spent countless hours redoing and then redoing again my models as I worked through them. I am deeply grateful for his patience and gifts to make this teaching a reality. Words can't express my gratitude to Barbara Law for the countless hours of editing she offered to the completion of Daily Habits of Intimacy with God. I am grateful for her and her husband Terry who shared wise counsel and insights to further my understanding to be more effective in sharing with you. I am grateful to Monica Epperson who helped move this teaching manual through the channels of copyright and preparing it for printing. Her dedication to this work has exceeded beyond what I could have asked for. I am thankful for my daughter, Cameron Coblentz, for sharing her amazing pictures. They offer beautiful illustrations of intimate places God has created. Then there are my prayer girls who pray with me and for me. Each one of you is a blessing to me. And last, but certainly not the least, is my husband Lloyd. He covered many bases on the home front to give me time to write. I am deeply grateful for his gentleness, kindness, and servant's heart.

Grace blessings to each one of you,
Roselene Coblentz

CONTENTS

Foreword

Those of us who have known Roselene Coblentz as a counselor or as a friend are thrilled to see the publication of this book. We have encouraged her for a long time to "duplicate" herself--that is, to share with others the insight, wisdom, and practical counsel that have led so many to healing and freedom. Each week of this Bible study sets a rich table of scriptural understanding and insight that Roselene has gleaned not only from her life, but from walking alongside the men and women she has helped to restore to new and rich lives in Christ. We are excited for you as you begin your journey with her in *Daily Habits of Intimacy with God.* You will be blessed and transformed!

Terry and Barbara Law
World Compassion/Terry Law Ministries

Roselene Coblentz is an amazing example of the purpose that is revealed in a redeemed story! Her personal experience and gift of counseling have been woven together to result in a powerful ministry to many. It is exciting to see her personal vision and mission expanded beyond her counseling practice to reach many more through this study. David L. Odom, executive director of Leadership Education at Duke Divinity, asserts that for transformation to occur there has to be activities, mindsets, and traits that are cultivated into habits. *Daily Habits of Intimacy with God* captures the essence of how to practically develop habits that lead to a discovery of Jesus and His power to transform and redeem our stories!

Holly Beitel
TRUE Stories Ministries & PurposeCast

Week One: Introduction to Your Intimacy Journey

Welcome to the beginning of your intimacy journey. I am so excited to share with you what God has shared with me over the last 30 years. In my relationship with God, I have worked these truths into my past and present life story. A deep and abiding intimacy with God has come as He has healed deep, childhood wounds. Over the years, as God and I have journeyed together it has also opened the way for healthier relationships and the fulfilling of my destiny. This is my desire for each of you. My prayer for you in this 12-week journey of "Daily Habits of Intimacy with God," is that you will experience Ephesians 3:14-21. I trust God will personally anchor you in the width, length, depth, and height of His great, eternal love for you. May you experience beyond your imagination intimacy of Him, healing of your wounds, and encounter acceptance and a deeper connection with others and then to love and serve others in your role in God's kingdom.

Whether you begin this journey alone or with a group, begin by processing these questions. How willing are you to risk being open and vulnerable in sharing the hidden parts of your internal world with another human being? With yourself? With God?

How often do you keep parts of you hidden: your dreams, desires, hurts, mistakes, sins, or struggles for fear of judgment or rejection?

How often do you share only parts of you, because other parts of you have a

● ● ●

Do Not Enter sign written on them, or they are locked away, and you don't believe you have the key to unlock them?

How many times can you remember when you have shared personal, private information of yourself and encountered judgment or rejection? We live in a society that values everyone for their performance. We are evaluated, appraised, judged, and ranked every day, even sometimes by those we love. We are under constant pressure therefore to perfect our performance. We believe a perfected performance equals greater acceptance. But who we are inside, our real self, goes into hiding. Because we fear rejection and judgment, we choose not to pursue intimacy, not to expose our inner self to another.

The ramifications of this loss of intimacy are great. The greatest loss is the true, real self. What is often left is a masked self, a facade, and often this is the only self we know; we even believe it to be the real, genuine self. Close relationships with others are also difficult, if not impossible, with a false self. Failure to really know ourselves, as God created us, creates conflict within us and within every other relationship. Until we return to God's original plan of intimacy, we cannot really know ourselves or live our lives as fully designed. We will not fulfill our destiny. I believe "Daily Habits of Intimacy with God" holds the key for the restoration of intimacy. Each week from your "sit place with Abba God" you will discuss a topic that will help you develop this intimacy, little by little, becoming the person God originally designed. Only God can enter into your past and restore it fully. Only He can connect your past to the present with redeeming grace for you and your relationships. Only He can provide you with a hopeful, promising future.

No journey is meant to be traveled alone. God desires others to join you on your journey, providing another source of knowing yourself. Through your relationships within your study group, God wants you to discover and share your real self, and to experience grace and acceptance that deepens intimacy. It is also a time to offer to others acceptance for them to develop intimacy with God. I have experienced many life stories with friends and clients who have stepped into the "intimacy journey" and have experienced amazing grace within their past and present, with healing for their hurts, restoration for their marriages and other relationships, and fulfillment of their destinies. Now is the time for you to begin your intimacy journey. Trust Him as He expresses personally what He will do for you: *You make known to me the path of life; you will fill me with joy in your presence, with eternal pleasures at your right hand (Psalm 16:11 NIV).* And

• • •

as He works His grace in you, may you fulfill your destiny in your God-given role in the kingdom as Paul shares: *However, I consider my life worth nothing to me; my only aim is to finish the race and complete the task the Lord Jesus has given me—the task of testifying to the good news of God's grace (Acts 20:24 NIV).*

Personal Growth Discussion

1. Share what your experience has been within your relationships from these three words:

   Trustworthy: Can I trust God and others? Can they trust me?

   Transparency: Can I share my real thoughts and feelings uncensoredly with God and others? Can they share with me?

   Acceptance: Do I feel loved and accepted by others when they share truthfully to me? Do they feel loved when I speak into their life?

2. What do you believe will challenge you the most in being committed to this 12-week journey?

Week Two: Your Sit Place with Abba God

The need for intimacy with God is at the very core of your being. All your beliefs and actions flow from this intimacy. Your intimate relationship with God determines the health of your own person and every one of your relationships. God desires that through your intimacy with Him you feel loved, accepted, valued, helped, strengthened, and encouraged. He wants you to know that every detail of your life matters to Him.

I have entitled the second week of this study "Your Sit Place with Abba God" to emphasize the necessity of setting aside time to be with Abba, Father God. Setting aside a specific time each day to give your undivided attention to God is the beginning of knowing Him intimately and understanding yourself more deeply in light of the One who made you.

If you were meeting with a friend or with your spouse to share time together or to encourage or be encouraged, you would not read a book in his or her presence. Nor, I hope, would you be texting on your phone or checking your email! The same is true in your relationship with Abba God. He desires you to come and sit with Him exclusively. He desires to listen to you as you share your heart and the stories of your life, while he expresses His care and comfort for you.

I use this phrase "sit place with God" to also call attention to the importance of establishing a place to be alone with God. Secure a quiet place: your favorite room, a favorite chair - any place where you can come quietly into

God's presence. You can also visually remember a special place you visited such as the beach, a mountain range, a waterfall, or a bench along a quiet path—returning there in your mind and welcoming God in that place.

What Happens in This "Sit Place with God?"

In your chosen place, meditate quietly, worshipping Him with your heart and giving thanks for His character, His actions, and His awesome love for you. Share your heart with Him and then listen to His heart. From this "sit place with Abba God" He will express His care for you and give you grace to do your day with Him. In this set aside time, you are present to God and He will become present to you in a real way. This is the foundation of a daily, intimate journey for a lifetime.

Our communion with God is a dialogue, not a monologue. This is not the time where you dump your problems on Him and walk away. This is not healthy for any relationship, much less your relationship with Abba God. In your "sit place with God," there is dual sharing and listening.

How Do I Hear from God? How Do I know it is God's Voice?

Many books have been written on this subject, several of which are mentioned in the resources at the end of this chapter. I want to give you something tangible to work with now and then encourage you to further your personal study.

The most important way God will speak to you is in your reading of Scripture. His Scriptures are His words to you. Often the Holy Spirit will make them jump off the page, highlight them for you, or He will bring them to your mind when you need encouragement or direction. For example, when you need encouragement He may share with you: *Trust Me at all times, pour out your heart to Me, I am your refuge (Psalm 62:8 NIV)*. Maybe you need wisdom in making a decision, and He shares with you: *To seek my wisdom is good. Ask Me. I will give to you generously (James 1:5 NIV)*.

I believe that you also can hear from your own language with God. Some may hear from a connection with nature, with music, or art; others from intellectual scholars of the past; still others may get words or pictures; and others may have dreams and visions. It is important to remember that what you hear as God's voice must always line up with the Word of God.

So along with your "sit place with Abba God," it is essential to read the Word of God. Regular, consistent reading of the Word allows you to recognize His voice and to know His will for your life. There are many excellent devotionals and Bible reading plans. Several are mentioned at the end of this chapter. Choose the plan that best suits you. Sitting with the God of Truth, nourishing yourself with His words of truth, God will personalize the devotional or Bible reading plan that you choose to speak to your personal and relational challenges.

An Important Note

Remember that your "sit place with Abba God" can occur throughout the day. In your heart, you can still access that quiet place from which you share your thoughts and feelings with God, and you can still hear His encouraging voice, no matter what you may be doing. This ability to "sit" with God, anytime or anywhere, is one of the most precious fruits of developing your daily "sit place with God." Come to him expecting that you will hear His voice.

Keeping a Journal

A journal is often helpful to write down what are you thinking and feeling during this time apart with God as well as what you believe He is saying to you. You can then refer back to God's personal words to you when the enemy comes to discourage, distract, or cause you to doubt. While you write, visualize Abba God sitting beside you, being attentive, and showing His love for you. This is personal, you and God.

Cheri's Journal

Here is a page from Cheri's journal that she keeps in her "sit place with God." She has been facing the challenge of her husband's job loss and her feelings of fear and anxiety. She chose to memorize and meditate on the words of David, writing them in her journal: *O my people, trust in him at all times. Pour out your heart to him, for God is our refuge (Psalms 62:8 NLT). You will keep in perfect peace all who trust in you, all whose thoughts are fixed on you! Trust in the Lord always, for the Lord God is the eternal Rock (Isaiah 26:3, 4 NLT).*

From Cheri's journal: God, you are my Lord God, my Eternal Rock. You are my Refuge. I desire to trust you. I am feeling desperate, discouraged, angry, and afraid. Why did this happen to us? What if he can't find a job and we can't pay our bills? We don't have very much in our savings to fall back on. I feel afraid and anxious all the time. But Abba God, you promise that you will keep me in perfect peace as I believe truthfully and trust you. You are trustworthy. I choose to trust you that you will provide a job for my husband and you will take care of our financial needs. My situation does matter to you. I will trust You now and forever, for You are the Lord, my Lord; You are the Rock eternal, my Rock eternal. In Jesus' name, Amen.

Cheri pauses and listens to His words to her. She continues to write in her journal, believing this is what God is speaking to her.

"Cheri, you are my daughter and all that concerns you matters to me. Your feelings of anxiety and your husband's job are important to me. I am here to help you. You can trust Me. Your husband will secure a job. In the meanwhile, trust me to care for your anxieties and for your needs. Do not be afraid. I will never leave you. You can count on Me. In my unfailing love for you, I will care for you and your husband. I will give you grace to pray for him, and to affirm and encourage him. Choose to believe in Me that I will provide and believe in him that he will secure a great job.

Brandon's Journal

Then there is Brandon who is struggling with addictions. He seeks God by reading Psalm 3-5.

Here is a page from his journal: "God, I keep trying to say no, but I repeatedly find myself returning to the internet. I feel so guilty and frustrated with myself. I attend a men's group, hoping it will help me. But I can't risk being open with them for fear they will think less of me. Lord, you are my shield and my help. I have to believe my deliverance comes from you. You will deliver me from my addictions. I need your blessing and grace on my life. God, you promise you will answer when I call you. You will help me and show me mercy. You are my God and I share my heart with you and wait in expectation. Lord God I take refuge in you. You spread your protection over me and surround me with your favor as a shield. You are my shield God Most High! I trust in You. You will help me to live free from all my addictions. You are my strength and help. I need you."

Brandon pauses and writes what he hears God share with him:

"Brandon, my son, I am with you. I am your shield. I hear your voice and your deliverance is in Me. I bless you with deliverance when you seek Me and come to Me. I am your refuge. Come and find your help and strength in Me. Deliverance from all your addictions is found in Me. You have My shield of protection and favor. You are My son and the light of My glory shines on you. You can trust Me. I will never fail you. My help is always available. I am your God and here to help you in your time of need. I will give you grace to say no to every temptation and yes to every true, pure, and good desire that will make you a strong and secure man."

Obedience

The final dimension of developing your "sit place with Abba God" is obedience—walking out whatever truth He speaks to your heart. Obedience is your response to being loved by God and receiving the words He speaks to you. John speaks straight forward to this truth: *I have loved you even as the Father has loved me. Remain in my love. When you obey my commandments,* you *remain in my love, just as I obey my Father's commandments and remain in his love (John 15:9, 10 NLT).* The truth is: love is obedience - obedience is love. Knowing His true, life-giving words and obeying every word He speaks is what deepens your intimacy with God, sets you free, and opens the way for powerful influence to others.

For Cheri, God gave her grace to pray for her husband, to affirm and encourage and believe in him. So rather than expressing her fear and anger to him all the time, she obeys God's words to her to affirm and uplift him. Brandon also takes the grace given by God and daily says no to each lure of the internet and each lie he has believed. He chooses to obey God's encouragement to spend time with Him, to be committed to a support group, and to grow his relationship with his wife.

Whatever challenges you are facing in your life right now, God wants to encourage you to go to your "sit place" where you can deepen your intimacy with Him and receive His help, encouragement, healing, hope, direction, or what you have need of in your life. He is waiting to welcome you and share time with you.

Abba God Model

It is important that all your struggles filter through your God relationship. He is the God who loves you and desires to hear your thoughts and feelings concerning you. Often it happens that when problems come, you are like a leapfrog and look for ways to fix your problems with your own mind. This type of "leapfrog practice" omits a relationship with God.

I encourage you to practice this model using a journal. Write your thoughts and feelings about a present or past event that you are dealing with. Pause and write what you hear God is saying back to you. Believe His true, pure words to you to care and comfort you. Then take His grace and obey what He says to you. As you dialogue with God, in all your circumstances, intimacy is developed. This is the best possible way of life. May it be your "daily" habit at the very core of your being in all of your life experiences. May God's love for you and your love for Him be the driving force of your life; everything else secondary to your intimacy with God.

ABBA GOD MODEL

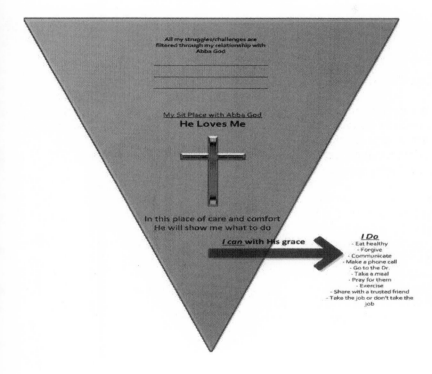

All my struggles/challenges are filtered through my relationship with Abba God

_____

_____

_____

My Sit Place with Abba God
He Loves Me

In this place of care and comfort
He will show me what to do

I can with His grace

I Do
- Eat healthy
- Forgive
- Communicate
- Make a phone call
- Go to the Dr.
- Take a meal
- Pray for them
- Exercise
- Share with a trusted friend
- Take the job or don't take the job

Roselene Coblentz, Ph.D, LMFT

Your Daily Habit of Prayer

Develop a daily habit of prayer. Prayer is relationship, built in your "sit place with God." You dialogue with Him personally; then listening, trusting, and obeying the words He speaks to you. You live internally/eternally first, and then it flows externally to those with whom you have influence.

Personal Growth Questions

1. How would you characterize your intimacy with God at this point in your spiritual journey? What do you struggle with that interferes with that intimacy? Be as honest as you can here.

2. Do you have a "sit place with Abba God?" What does it look like physically, visually? If you are not as consistent about going there as you would like, commit yourself this week to sitting with God each day. If you do not have a "sit place," find one this week and go there consistently throughout the week to be with God.

3. What area of your life do you need to share with God and hear about from Him? Do you have any "Do Not Enter" signs in your internal life you want God to remove?

4. If you do not already journal, bring a journal or pad of paper to your "sit place" and write down the thoughts and feelings you are sharing with God, and then write what you believe He is saying to you.

5. At the end of the week, write down what you have experienced during this "sit place with God." Are there any areas God has pinpointed in which He is asking you to obey or to change? How do you feel your relationship with God has grown?

Prayer

God, you are my God. You are Good. You are good to me. Put in me a desire to place You above all others. Fill me with a longing for You - to hunger and thirst for You. I want to see You, Your power and glory in my life. I need Your unfailing love to come and embrace me. From my sit place with You, teach me to worship and praise Your name. Allow Your goodness to meet me there in that place. You are my Strength, my Refuge, and my Helper. Come satisfy and sustain me with Your presence throughout the day and into the night. It is Your desire that I not only know You love me, but that I feel Your love. My life matters to You, every joy and struggle. I choose You, for Your strong-loving arms hold me securely. I trust You with all of my daily circumstances, for You are trustworthy. I will share with You all that concerns me and trust that You will listen and guide me. You love me and I love You! Mark my life with intimacy with You as You are Perfect and Eternal Love. In Jesus Name, Amen (Psalm 63).

* * *

Resources

The Bible (in your favorite translation)
How to Develop a Powerful Prayer Life, Dr Gregory R Frizzell
The Lost Art of Practicing the Presence of the Lord, Jim Goll
Quiet Time Bible Guide, Cindy Bunch (365 days through the New Testament and Psalms)
Hearing the Voice of God by Steve Sampson
The Ultimate Voice by Oral Roberts

Notes...

Week Three: Your Truth-Life Preserver

Welcome to Week Three. I trust that you have begun your intimacy journey from your "sit place with Abba God." I hope you are experiencing a new depth of relationship with Him.

This week's focus is on truth.

Truth is like a life preserver. The purpose of a life preserver, of course, is to prevent drowning. If you are sent plunging into stormy waters, you will hang onto that life preserver because your life depends on it.

Truth is every bit as essential to your well-being. Without truth at the core of your being and your belief system, you are vulnerable to distortions and deceptions. And when life throws you into an emotional, raging sea, truth will be your life preserver while you are waiting for rescue.

Three truths are fundamental to establish a solid foundation of truth:

1) God is the author of truth: *Into Your hand, I commit my spirit, O God of Truth (Ps. 31, NIV).*

2) He wants you to know the truth about His love for you and to know yourself in light of it: He *desires truth in the inner parts (Ps. 51:6, NIV).*

3) Knowing the truth will liberate you from the lies and deceptions which oppress you and hinder you from fulfilling your God-given destiny: *The truth*

will set you free (John 8:32, NIV).

The God of Truth

Scripture says, *It is impossible for God to lie (Hebrews 6:18, NIV).* Every word God speaks is true, so you can trust Him to lead you safely and wisely through life's twists and turns. Truth is very powerful, whether you believe it or not. Truth believed is life-changing. A lie, on the other hand, has no power until you believe it, but when you do, it will usually distort your view of yourself, or others, or God. This is why it is imperative to know and trust the God of Truth.

Truth in the Inner Parts

"He loves me and desires to have personal, intimate relationship with me" is the most powerful truth that God wants you to believe. It is God's heart that you would experience His great love as the foundation to all other truth. *See what great love the Father has lavished on us, that we should be called children of God! And that is what we are! This is how we know what love is: Jesus Christ laid down his life for us. And we ought to lay down our lives for our brothers and sisters. Dear children, let us not love with words or speech but with actions and in truth. This is how we know that we belong to the Truth and how we set our hearts at rest in His presence (1 John 3:1, 16, 18, 19, NIV).* It is essential that you daily activate this greatest of all truths, "He loves me," by inviting this truth into the core of your person.

Set Free by Truth

The divine purpose of believing truth is to be set free! Remember, thinking or confessing truth is not the same as believing truth at the core of your person. The exchange of faulty believing for truthful believing in the inner parts will help you become healthier mentally and emotionally, make constructive, positive choices, and develop meaningful relationships.

As you believe the truth that matches God's truth, that truth will change your behavior over time. What you believe is what you will do! The highest purpose to believing truthfully is to bring permanence of change, whether that is to leave behind depression, anxiety, addiction, anger, fear, worry, negativity, or whatever your challenge is. Do not stop; do not give up until you arrive at the door of "set free," which then opens to a door of opportunity for your greater growth.

Ashley's Story

Many of your life experiences come as an unpredicted storm in the dark of night. One of these blew into Ashley's life when postpartum depression occurred after the birth of her daughter. Within a few months she was diagnosed with major depression. For three years it had a death grip on her. The medical community did what they could, but after two 30-day hospitalizations, two electrotherapy procedures, and 13 different antidepressants, their final word to her was depression would be her permanent challenge.

Ashley knew that she could not continue in the clutches of depression and stay earth bound. By divine intervention, she began a truth journey with a psychologist. The journal she kept revealed countless self-defeating lies that had traveled with her as friends for years. Event by event, day by day, from her "sit place with Abba God," she began to replace them with truth. The major lies she had embraced were: I am unlovable, I am worthless, I am unacceptable, and there's no hope for me.

Slowly Ashley began to replace these lies with: my life has purpose and meaning, I am valued because I am created by God and the works of Christ make me worthy and acceptable. The greatest truth of all: I am loved by God, family, and friends. What defines me is not what has happened to me, but what I believe, and my response to those truths matters most of all.

Little by little, defriending the lies, truth began to find its way to Ashley's heart. Three months later, suicidal-depression moved out for good, all ties to it severed. Now almost 30 years later, truth continues to be her lifetime companion. Journeying with truth opened the way to personal healing, healthier relationships, and the fulfilling of her God-given destiny.

Everyday Thoughts

As children journey through life, fears and insecurities enter in through hurt and pain. Each of those experiences is linked to an unconscious thought. These thoughts go undetected because children lack the ability to process them cognitively and are more connected to what they feel, thus believing that what they feel must be true. In addition, parents are often more focused on appropriate behaviors versus giving consideration to what their child may believe internally. Therefore, these messages move from childhood to adulthood becoming what I call *everyday thoughts*.

* * *

These everyday thoughts are also known as your self-talk; and if distorted, they usually take the form of your negative I am's, I cannot's, what if's, and should or shouldn't statements. Some examples: I am unlovable, I am undeserving, I am unworthy, I can't succeed at anything, I can never trust again, I cannot forgive, what if I fail?, what if he leaves?, she should not have left me, he should be more helpful, they should have been more responsible.

Often under the influence of fear and insecurity, these everyday thoughts, faulty and negative, are accepted as "truth." From this distortion of truth, you develop a faulty belief system about your personal life and relationships, and adopt faulty premises from which you make life decisions, marring both your present and future. It is important to recognize that if this faulty believing is at the core of your life, it will be reflected in unhealthy, negative, and destructive emotions, behaviors, and choices. Put another way, when you are engaged in destructive or negative behaviors, you can be sure there is faulty self-talk or lies behind them. Therefore, to live lives of healthy well-being, it is crucial to exchange these distortions for truthful believing.

Janet and Mike's Story

Janet has been married for five years to Mike, who frequently is out of town on business. As a stay-at-home mom, she usually finds herself parenting alone their two-year-old twins. She views her marriage as two roommates living very separate lives. Janet attempts to communicate to Mike the importance of nurturing their relationship, and he agrees, but no change occurs. Even when he returns home, he is still preoccupied with work projects and is not attentive to Janet or their children. Mike struggles inwardly with the conflict of balancing his work demands with time for his marriage and children. They are both increasingly aware that they have created distance by not affirming, encouraging, and taking the time needed for each other.

Janet remembers feeling overwhelmed, scared, and lonely while growing up without a dad as her mom worked two jobs and Janet was responsible for her younger sibling. Mike recalls his dad always working, and he and his brother always being with mom. He missed his dad and wanted him to be at his baseball games, but his mom was the only one cheering him on.

Both Mike and Janet remembered from pre-marital counseling the importance of self-talk. Recalling that their emotions are tied to their thinking, they began to consider what they were telling themselves and what they were believing. Some of the lies they wrestled with included: I am not good enough, I am overwhelmed, I am insecure, I can't change, I can't quit, what if I make a mistake, what if I fail, he/she should be more considerate, life is too hard.

Gradually, Janet and Mike challenged their self-talk, exchanging their lies for truth: I am good enough because of the work of Christ; I can care for my feelings in a healthy way, I am secure in Christ who loves me and desires to have relationship with me; I can change with the help of Christ and others; there is no mistake or failure God cannot redeem; I can do my life well with the help of God, even if someone is inconsiderate or disappoints me; desiring a loving marriage is good, and I can let go of expectations and demands; life is challenging, but with the help of God and others, I can embrace the good of every challenge for my personal growth and my marriage.

They each began to value their "sit time" with God, receiving His boundless love and acceptance. Their marriage was strengthened as they allowed God to share His truth, replacing their faulty thinking.

Assess Your Self-Talk

It is important to assess your everyday thoughts about yourself or others in your self-talk. Too often faulty thoughts will enter in, and you find yourself reacting in ways you didn't intend or are destructive. It is important to train yourself, when your emotions begin to escalate, to stop and ask yourself, "What am I believing or telling myself here?" Ask the Holy Spirit to put His finger on the untruth you are believing. So begin by eavesdropping on yourself! Is it really true that you are "never going to amount to much?" Is it really true that you are not as good/smart/beautiful/successful as your sister/brother? Is it really true that you are always going to be taken advantage of?

The vital question you must ask yourself is: do my thoughts match God's thoughts? As you believe the truth that matches God's truth, that truth will change your behavior over time. What you believe is what you will do!

Truth Model:

Write down a present event you are facing. List your feelings about that challenge. Scale them from 0-10, 10 being the highest intensity. For example, anxiety 8, depressed 6, frustrated 5. Note that 0-4 is considered the norm; in other words, others experiencing this life event could be expected to have similar feelings within this range. There is nothing magical about the numbers; they just help you to know what feelings to give further attention to in your self-talk. If your feelings score above 4 (5+), they may be connected to faulty thinking, and/or from unresolved feelings from childhood, death of a friend, loss of a job, or former marriage, etc. Write down your thoughts that connect to your negative feelings about this situation. List your behaviors that are connected to these negative feelings and thoughts. Write down what the results will be if you continue this pattern of thinking and behavior.

Here is an example for you to follow. *Event:* partner threatening to leave again. *Thoughts* (self-talk): "What if he leaves again? I can't deal with it." *Feelings*: insecure, afraid, and anxious. *Behavior:* withdrawn, emotionally shut down, and insomnia. This pattern will result in the neglect of using your voice in sharing your thoughts, feelings, and desires; which could lead to resolving the issue or at least there would be no regret in not expressing yourself.

Truth Exchange: *Thoughts* (self-talk): I can only be responsible for my decisions. If he leaves, God and others will help me through the situation. I am never alone." *Feelings:* hopeful and supported. *Behaviors:* engaging, open, and communicative. This pattern will be constructive and positive with hope of healing the relationship.

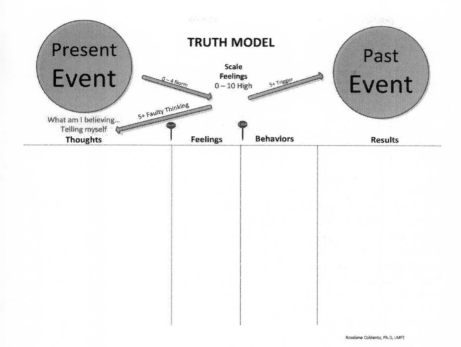

TRUTH MODEL

Present Event

Past Event

Scale
Feelings
0 – 10 High

0 – 4 Norm

5+ Trigger

5+ Faulty Thinking

What am I believing...
Telling myself

Thoughts | **Feelings** | **Behaviors** | **Results**

Roselene Coblentz, Ph.D, LMFT

Your Daily Habit of Truth

Develop a daily habit of truth. From your sit place, assess your everyday thoughts, replacing faulty self-talk to match God's thoughts. Believing truthfully is displayed powerfully in what you *do* personally and relationally.

Personal Growth Questions

1. What truths are most important to you? Truths that you hold on to every day as your truth life preserver?

2. Ask God to show you any lies you may believe and write them down.

3. Next to each of those lies, write down what truths you need to believe. Replace the lie with the truth.

4. Share a difficult event from your past. What thoughts and feelings do you have about it? What thoughts are lies? Write down what truths are needed to replace them.

5. Ask God to help you "listen in" this week to your own self-talk. Ask Him to pinpoint untrue thoughts and to replace them with His thoughts. In your journal write down what God shows you.

Prayer

God, You are my God. You are The God of Truth. I desire Your Truth at the core of my being. Starting with, You love me, You really love me. Secure that truth in the core of my being. Let me live my whole life from this great, eternal truth. I want Your Truth, for it is only Your Truth that will set me free from all my lies. I choose to exchange every lie for Your Truth. I desire to love Your true and pure words and meditate on them all day and all night long. May they become sweeter than honey to me as You work them into my heart. I want Your Truth to be my lamp that lights my path day and night; so I can see where I am going one step at a time. I place my hope in your Truthful words to me. All Your words to me are true! I trust in Your truthful words to me for You are Trustworthy. Mark my life with truth as You are Truth. In Jesus Name, Amen.
(Ps. 31:5, Ps. 51:6, John 8:32; Psalms 119:97, 103, 105, 114, 147-148, 160)

● ● ●

Resources

The Bible
Telling Yourself the Truth, Dr William Backus
Self Talk-Soul Talk, Jennifer Rothchild, Robin McGraw
Change Your Brain, Change Your Life, Dr. Daniel Amen

Notes...

Week Four: Your Grace Place

This week you will focus on God's Grace, the foundation for understanding God's love and activity in your life.

Grace is a gift from God to you. It is often defined as God's unmerited favor. God's grace demands nothing from you, but to believe and receive how deeply He loves you. Grace, partnering with Truth, is nothing short of revolutionary! *The law was given through Moses, but grace and truth came through Jesus Christ (John 1:17, NKJV).*

Grace is one of the most misunderstood and misrepresented truths. Grace is not permissiveness about sin—do your own thing, flippantly say I'm sorry, and then repeat the pattern. Nor do you receive Grace as a result of your own efforts or Christian practices.

If your efforts are not needed, how then do you receive this gift of love, the undeserved favor of God? I hope you are asking this question because the answer is vital to your understanding of Grace.

Grace Defined

God sacrificially gave His One and Only Son, Jesus, who had no sin, to pay the price for your sin. *All have sinned and come short of the glory of God (Romans 3:23, NIV).* Jesus took the punishment for our wrongdoing so you and I can come before God without condemnation.

• • •

Paul confirms this truth: *For God made Christ, who never sinned, to be the offering for our sin, so that we could be made right with God through Christ (2 Corinthians 5:21, NLT).* This is the only way you can enter into the presence of God, for God is holy and just and cannot look upon sin without judgment. He sent His own Son to die upon a cross to bear your rightful punishment, so you could come before Him without blame.

The prophet Isaiah states: *There is no other God but me, a just God and a Savior (Isaiah 45:21, NKJV).* As Bible teacher Derek Prince once explained, God's justice and God's mercy are like two sides of one coin. On one side is God's justice and on the other is His mercy. God's justice is an absolute standard: it is objective, judging everyone impartially; and it is exact, that is, unvarying in its demand for perfect righteousness. God's perfect justice does not allow for "pretty close" or thinking you are "more righteous" than someone else. God's justice is unvarying and perfect: you and I do not want God's justice.

But the other side of the coin is God's mercy. Because sin entered the world and therefore entered every one of us, God knew we would fall far short of holiness. You and I will never be able to live perfectly, no matter how hard we try. So God Himself provided the solution; in Jesus Christ you have a Savior who has satisfied the perfect standard of God's justice. *[He] Himself bore our sins in His own body on the tree, that we, having died to sin, might live for righteousness (1 Peter 2: 24, NKJV).*

In Him we have mercy. As the scripture says, *Mercy and truth have met together; righteousness and peace have kissed (Psalm 85:10, NKJ V).* And because Jesus has satisfied his Father's justice, by taking upon Himself our punishment, *we can come boldly unto his throne of grace in time of need (Hebrews 4:16).*

Now that we have defined grace, how do we receive it?

Grace Received

Of all the major religions in the world, only Christianity declares that God's love is unconditional. The Buddhists, Hindus, Jews, and Muslims all offer a way to earn approval. The Bible clearly teaches that God's grace is unconditional, but it also teaches you that you are responsible for determining how much grace you walk in. In James 4:6, James says, *But he gives **more** grace. Therefore,* he says, *God resists the proud, but gives grace* *to the humble.* The key to walking in Grace is to learn how to humble yourself.

How do you humble yourself? There are many ways you can humble yourself: when you walk gratefully before God, grace flows from your thanksgiving. When you give sacrificially, whether it be your time, talent, or treasure, grace flows from your giving. The third and most difficult way of humbling yourself is to forgive those who have wounded you. We will look much more closely at this aspect next week.

First Dimension of Grace

With these truths in place, I want you to reflect on Grace within its two life-giving dimensions: the Grace that does for you that which you cannot do for yourself, and then the grace God gives you to do that which only you can do in response. These are two separate facets, but linked by the initiative of God's great love to you and your love response to Him. You are fully loved and accepted apart from any of your doings, but you are free to choose to love Him back and obey Him. *As the Father loved Me, I also have loved you; abide in My love. If you keep My commandments, you will abide in My love, just as I have kept My Father's commandments and abide in His love (John 15:9, 10 NKJV).* If Jesus gave you His life as expressed by John, *This is how we know what love is: Jesus Christ laid down His life for us (I John 3:16, NKJV).* How could you not love Him back in your obedience? Let your thoughts meditate on this. Just remember it is not love if forced against your will. Therefore, God loves you unconditionally. Yet, He desires that you love Him back. This is also true in your human relationships. You can love others, but you cannot force them to love you back. You can desire their love, but it is important to free them up to love you back in their choosing.

Most of us have been so conditioned to" performance love" that we cannot really embrace the possibility that no matter how I choose to live my life, Grace in the love of God is always present; that He loves me with no strings attached. Because of your conditioning, you become resistant and revert back to trying to earn the love of God or doing something to deserve that love. But that is the good news of the gospel. God does not ask you to change or do anything before He loves you. He does not ask you to change or do anything to keep on loving you. He chooses to love you, His Grace fully capturing you, that then and only then, your response would be to love Him back with the Grace He gives to you. Even *Merriam-Webster's* defines grace as effortless beauty, ease of movement, pleasing quality, favor, divine love and protection, virtue, and *strength to choose to do all that is required of you*. All of these are found in God's Grace. Here are a few examples of embracing the beauty of Grace. May they find their way to your understanding: Grace requires nothing of you but believing truthfully and receiving fully His Grace. I want to remind you that this is the result of God's sacrificial love of His Son that you can welcome this Grace. And then respond back in love with your obedience.

The Beauty of Grace

You receive Grace in its effortless beauty like welcoming the morning fresh air on a brisk walk. There is no work involved. There is only breathing deeply the air of His great, eternal love into your lungs and hearts.

You receive Grace in its ease of movement like welcoming a tender, nurturing embrace of a loving mother. There is no work involved. There is only the receiving of all the favor and good in nurture that comes from His affectionate care for your heart.

You receive Grace in all its divine work as the loving kindness and protectiveness of a father watching over his little brood. There is no work involved. There is only you enjoying the protective care and strong, loving arms of Abba God.

Grace in its greater beauty is receiving Christ the Gift, the treasure from The Lord. There is no work involved. There is only believing the truth and receiving the gift of Grace in Christ Jesus in all of His glory that is revealed in your eternal belonging to Him, and being loved by Him.

Grace in all its strength is giving His Grace-sufficiency for your weakness. In this Grace, there is the work of joining His Grace with your will. There is only the beauty of strength in partnering with Grace to do what pleases Him, loving Him back in your obedience. All of these aspects of Grace are what God does for you, without your effort.

Karl's Story

Karl was beginning to learn this Grace journey. In the past, as a young adult, he got up early every morning to read his Bible and pray for others. It was a valued discipline of how he lived his life, but it lacked the relational dimension of Grace to him. He was more focused on what he did for God than what God had done for him or continued to do for him daily through the death and resurrection of Jesus. But Karl began a feel a growing dissatisfaction within himself, a growing hunger. He wanted to really know God. Slowly, he began to anticipate his early morning time because he was meeting with God and the Presence of Jesus. Karl, now at the age of 55, was entering for the first time into the Grace realm of being loved, valued, and humbled through the works of Jesus. His discipline of studying the Scriptures, praying for others, and serving them became secondary to his time with God. These actions began to grow out of his response to being fully loved and accepted by the God of all Grace.

Second Dimension of Grace

The second dimension of Grace is receiving His Grace to do what only you can do. You choose to respond in obedience, aligning your will with His Grace. To begin this grace relationship, it is imperative that you center yourself from the position of "He is my all-sufficient Grace:" *By the grace of God I am what I am (I Corinthians 15:10, NKJV).* From this center, you build a strong, personal relationship based on the words and works of Christ. There is nothing of yourself, only what He has done for you.

Following the next story, I have listed some important Scriptures. I realize how easy it is to read and know the Scriptures with your intellect only. There is often little argument that you believe them to be true, but your choices and responses to challenges often reflect you only believe with your head. I challenge you when you are struggling with difficult situations to filter them through these scriptural truths, moving them from your head to your heart in your personal relationship with God.

Kacie's Story

Kacie, age 22, started to practice these truths as she faced her medical diagnosis of a brain tumor. Daily in her "sit place with God," she reminded herself of His truth, "He loves me and will work all things out for my good." She chose to trust that He would give her daily strength and provide for her every financial need. On days when Kacie was too weak to get out of bed, tears flowing down her face, she saw herself being held secure in God's strong, loving arms. She knew she couldn't earn this love and was desperately dependent on it. In His love for her, she felt the Presence of Jesus strengthening her each day. She trusted Him to send her all the help and support she needed from others. Though often weak and discouraged, she trusted His perfect love to face all her fears, believing His love would sustain her.

Here is her repeated heart prayer: "God, you love me with Your eternal love. I center myself in your everlasting, strong love for me. I choose to trust that you will work every detail out in my life, including my finances and the help I need daily. I will trust your strong, loving arms of love to be my help and strength on the days I don't believe I can push myself any further, desiring to give up. I embrace all Your love to me because of Your gift to me in Jesus. You are my Strength and Help. You are Perfect Love to me and you will move out all my fears as I meditate on Your love and care for me. I will give thanks that You are always with me."

In response, Kacie hears God's voice reminding her, "I am here for you, I will never leave you. You can count on Me. I will hold you close to me day and night. Do not fear; I will help you. My love will sustain you in your darkest days. All My grace is here for you in the Presence of Jesus to provide all the help you need. My grace is all-sufficient."

Meditate on these Scriptures:

• *God works all things for the good of those who love Him. (Romans 8:28)*

• *It is God who works in you. (Philippians 2:13)*

• *He works in you His grace so you can will and act for His good purpose. (Philippians 2:13)*

• *You can do everything because you are "in Christ" who strengthens you. (Philippians 4:13)*

• *God of all Grace…will himself restore you and make you strong, firm and steadfast. (1 Peter 5:10)*

• *You have "eternal redemption" (Hebrews 9:12): washed, sanctified, and justified in the name of the Lord Jesus Christ and by the Spirit of your God. (I Corinthians 6:11)*

Because of these truths, you also can declare truthfully your relationship with God is secure by Grace:

• *Christ saves you; it is a gift from God, not by works. (Ephesians 2:8, 9)*

• *Christ, God incarnate came in human form: lived-died-lives to save completely, interceding for you; sitting at the right hand of God. (Romans 5:8, Hebrews 7:24-25)*

• *There is nothing you can do to stop Christ being offered to you, to stop His love for you. (Romans 8:32)*

Finally, you can declare truthfully your "I am's" by Grace:

• *I am created in the image of God. (Genesis 1:27)*

• *I am purchased by the blood of the Lamb. (I Peter 1:18, 19)*

• *I am loved. I am valued. I am secure. I am accepted. I am forgiven. (Jeremiah 3:31, I Corinthian 6:11, I Peter 5:10, I John 1:9)*

• *God desires to have personal, intimate relationship with me. (John 14:9-11; John 17:20- 23)*

• *He desires that I experience His great love: its breadth, length, height, and depth. (Ephesians 3:17-21)*

God is a relational God. He created you in His image to have a love relationship with you. Your desires for relationship come from Him. He died that He could win you back and again have relationship with you. You have nothing to do with this love, except to believe the truth of it and receive His Grace. From the desires of His own heart, God decided to love you and to enjoy an intimate relationship with you. Thus in our obedience, joining your will with His Grace, you can make good on His grace in your responses to daily events.

Grace Model

God designed that your first understanding of grace would be within the family structure. The love you receive from your parents, apart from your behavior, would be your first experience of grace to yourself. Family love is to be a representation of God's love and grace to you. The love parents are intended to express to their children is not performance based, but love for the child as a person, a human being. Children believe and receive this love and grow up in this nurturing realm of loving parents. Like the unconditional love of God, there is no fear of loss of that love. Because of human nature, however, parents' love is conditional. But by the grace of God, parents still choose to love their children as unconditionally as possible. They offer a grace realm that their children can trust and grow in, believing this grace will always be present, no matter their choices or behaviors. God desires that children would feel loved, valued, secure, safe, accepted, forgiven, and experience trustworthiness within the parent-child relationship. This experience was meant to create a sense of belonging, centering them in grace.

This plan of God is challenged when grace moves from a focus on loving the person to behavior-based love. Children naturally desire to perform, please, perfect, and pretend within their childish imagination. It is worth noting here that your human nature does come with tendencies of selfishness and rebellion. But for my purposes here I want to focus on the problem that occurs when parents do not separate love/acceptance for the child apart from his or her behaviors. Children then move from childhood to adulthood with the perception: "my performance equals my acceptance." And as a society, within our schools, churches, work places, and other organizations, the pattern of performance continues to be deeply entrenched into adulthood. Thus the belief system becomes ingrained that "pleasing performance" is required even if I have to pretend and is what provides the love and acceptance desired. The final stage in this process occurs when the child transfers what he or she has learned from his parents to God: "God's acceptance of me is based on my performance." This belief is easily accepted: to get God to love me, I must keep on perfecting, performing, pleasing, and pretending. This pattern of thinking directs all of your other relationships as well. Therefore, all of your life experiences are filtered through a ME filter. Being loved and accepted is all about Me perfecting, Me pleasing, Me performing, and Me pretending.

GRACE MODEL

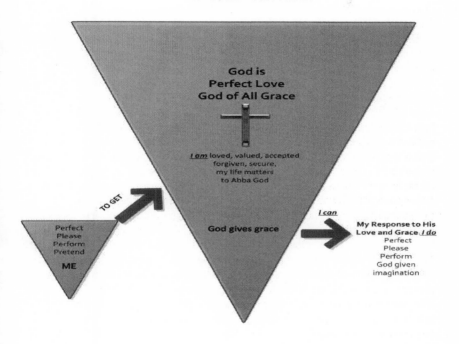

Roselene Coblentz, Ph.D, LMFT

Your Daily Habit of Dual Grace

Develop the daily habit of "dual" Grace. From your sit place, trust the God of all Grace to do for you what you cannot do for yourself, and making good on the grace of God to do what is yours to do as He speaks it to you.

It is imperative for the ME filter to be replaced with the HE LOVES ME Grace filter. All of your experiences and challenges need to be filtered through the truth of "He Loves Me." Remember that this love is centered in God's sacrifice of His Son which has secured for you an intimate relationship with Him. Within this grace relationship, He will redeem and restore you; making you strong, secure, steady, and sure. He gives you grace to believe truthfully, to forgive, and heals every hurt spiritually, emotionally, and physically.

Sally's Story

Sally remembers the 10 years of embracing the 4 P's: pleasing, perfecting, performing, and pretending to be "Christian" in all the ways that she believed would deliver acceptance and love from God and others. She spent years in church attendance, involvement in women's Bible studies, and maintaining an exterior that says "I am all-together" to secure acceptance. Sally knew little of the rest (quiet and peace) that comes from receiving the gift of Grace in Christ. Little by little, however, she began to grasp the truth: He loves me. No matter the challenge, Sally did not let go of this truth. Centering her life daily in "He loves me" encouraged her to filter all of her challenges within this Grace relationship. It is in this Grace-secured, trusted relationship with God that she continues to experience feeling loved, valued, safe, secure, forgiven, and accepted as she allows her heart to heal from life's disappointments. Sally values waking each morning, feeling loved by God and believing there isn't anything that she can do or not do that would stop His caring for her heart.

Personal Growth Questions

1. Describe what love and acceptance looked like in your family of origin.

2. Which of the 4 P's (pleasing, perfecting, performing, pretending) do you fall back on the most to secure love and acceptance from God and others?

3. What do you think most blocks your receiving God's Grace – His unconditional gift of love and favor in your life?

4. Describe one challenge you are currently facing. How might that situation change if you looked at it less through the ME Filter, and more through the He Loves Me/Grace Filter?

5. What is God speaking to you to do to make good on His grace?

Prayer

God, You are Perfect Love. You are Mercy. You are the God of all Grace. You are the Redeemer. My heart is humbled that Jesus who never sinned and I who sin all the time that You became my sin covering. You suffered and died for me. God, my heart is grateful that You showed me mercy, love, and grace. You forgave me, raised me up, and positioned me in Jesus Christ. Thank You for Your kindness in Your gift to me in Jesus. I did not do anything to deserve this gift. It is Your gift to me because of Your deep love for me and Your desire to have relationship with me. Your Word tells me that this gift was purchased by the blood of Christ, the sinless, spotless, Lamb of God. I am deeply humbled. My heart is forever grateful. I choose to attach my will with Your amazing grace and obey You with my heart. Mark me with Grace as only You can as the God of all Grace. In Jesus Name, Amen. (Ephesians 2:4-10 NKJV; 1 Peter 1:18-19 NLT)

Resources

He Loves Me, Wayne Jacobsen
Because He Loves Me, Elyse M. Fitzpatrick
Grace Works, Dudley Hall
Embracing the Love of God, James Bryan Smith
What's So Amazing about Grace? Phil Yancey

Notes...

Week Five: Your Gift of Forgiveness

Welcome back. This week from your "sit place with God" you will consider your beliefs about forgiveness, why you need to forgive, who you need to forgive, and how. Forgiveness is one of the most powerful experiences of God's grace and healing, and opens the door to greater intimacy with Him.

Leslie's Story

Leslie wrote in her journal, "My hurt is so great I can hardly breathe. To forgive—I can't even imagine what that would look like." She had been sexually abused by her grandfather as a young child. Though she is 29, her pain is as real as though it happened yesterday. Leslie struggles to feel any hope of experiencing forgiveness, healing, or giving herself permission to grieve her childhood losses.

She continues to write in her journal, "God, I ask you to center me in your love, as I sit in my favorite chair, knowing you sit with me. I want to feel your love wrapped around me, Your warmth and protectiveness, driving all my fears out of my mind and heart." Leslie is still mulling over the words of her devotional a few days earlier, *Forgive as the Lord forgave you (Colossians 3:13, NKJV)*. She values all the ways the Lord forgives her daily, but forgiving her grandfather seems far beyond her abilities.

The Truth about Forgiveness

As always, you must approach forgiveness from the foundation of truth.

What does God's word tell us about forgiveness?

First, you have been forgiven by God. *All have sinned,* Paul tells us in Romans 3:23, or as John says, *If we claim to be without sin, we deceive ourselves and the truth is not in us (1 John1:8, NKJV).* As we discussed last week, because God is holy and just, He cannot look on our sin without judgment. But because of His great love, God provided a way to satisfy His own justice: He sent to earth His Son, *who Himself bore our sins in His own body on the tree, that we, having died to sins, might live for righteousness (1 Pet. 2:24, NKJV).*

I pray you will give much thought to this precious truth: your forgiveness is only possible because of Christ's shed blood for you. God has cleansed, washed, and sanctified you by the blood of Jesus, opening the way for you to enter into fellowship with God. As you daily embrace His forgiveness by the blood of the Lamb, you will begin to find healing for your heart and also begin the journey to forgiving others.

How does your forgiveness tie in to forgiving those who have wounded you?

Again, we must turn to Scripture for truth. Paul writes in Colossians, *Bear with each other and forgive whatever grievances you may have against one another. Forgive as the Lord forgave you (Col 3:13, NIV).* Or this passage from Ephesians, *Be kind and compassionate to one another forgiving each other, just as in Christ God forgave you (Ephesians 4:32, NIV). God was reconciling the world to himself in Christ, not counting men's sins against them. And he has committed to us the message of reconciliation (2 Cor. 5:19, NIV).*

Why is Forgiveness So Difficult?

The scriptural requirement is plain—why then is forgiveness often so difficult?

The answer is two-fold. First, because you and I believe that the wrong deserves punishment; we cannot just let this person "off the hook." Forgiving the person seems to be letting him or her off scot-free. He doesn't deserve to get away with that! She doesn't deserve to get off so easily! In other words, we have set ourselves up as their judge. Do not misunderstand me—the wrongs some of us experienced have been very grievous indeed, and we have suffered deeply as a result. But Scripture does not say there is a sliding scale of forgiveness. We are called to forgive *everyone* who has harmed us.

● ● ●

When we hang on to the sense of grievance we feel, it isn't long before the resentment turns into bitterness. Scripture is also clear about what happens to us when bitterness takes hold in our lives. The writer of Hebrews says, *See to it that no one misses the grace of God and that no bitter root grows up to cause trouble and defile many (Hebrews 12:15, NIV)*. At the root of bitterness is a longing for revenge. Scripture responds to this human impulse as well: *Beloved, do not avenge yourselves...for it is written, 'Vengeance is Mine, I will repay, says the Lord'...Do not be overcome by evil, but overcome evil with good (Romans12:19, NKJV)*.

In the discussion of grace last week, I mentioned that grace flows more freely in our lives when we humble ourselves. Forgiving requires such a humbling. You must lay aside your demand for punishment and submit to God's word to forgive. Releasing that person who has harmed you will bring you release. And it also will release a flow of God's grace in your life you have not yet experienced. Failure to do so, to harbor bitterness instead, will impede God's grace and imprison you. That's why Scripture says, *The merciful man doeth good to his own soul (Proverbs 11:17, NIV)*.

Another reason why forgiveness is often difficult is that forgiveness involves facing the hurt you have experienced. Denying or repressing the hurt is not the same thing as forgiveness, nor is pretending that what happened is "no big deal." Usually these hurts have only gone underground where they are still causing pain and anger and even self-pity. These feelings are often expressed in hurtful behaviors towards others. So true forgiveness means facing the often painful reality of what was done to you—or perhaps what you did to another. God gives grace for this part of the process as well.

Forgiveness is a choice. When you choose to forgive, your decision releases the grace of God to flow in that situation. I encourage you, in your "sit place with God," to humble yourself before God, acknowledge those people you need to forgive, and receive His grace to forgive them.

You may also need to forgive yourself. God does not want you to be "on the hook" either. In your sit place with Abba God, tell him what you need to be forgiven for, and you will receive His gracious forgiveness.

Forgiving God

I cannot pass on here without saying that the trail of our unforgiveness often leads to God Himself. Though many of us would not admit this, because we do love God, deep in our hearts we often hold Him responsible for what happened to us—for allowing that hurtful or even evil thing to occur, to blight our lives. Where were you, God? There is not room enough here, of course, to take on the subject of why God allows suffering, and there are no easy answers. You may need to "forgive" God. Tell Him that right now you do not understand why He let that happen to you, but you forgive Him for what seems like a terrible injustice. Acknowledge that you cannot fully understand His purposes, but what happened hurt you deeply. Tell Him that you want to lay down your anger towards Him and receive His love.

If I Could Sit With You Awhile
By MercyMe

When I cannot feel, when my wounds don't heal
Lord I humbly kneel, hidden in You
Lord, You are my life so I don't mind to die
Just as long as I am hidden in You

If I could just sit with You a while, if You could just hold me
Nothing could touch me though I'm wounded, though I die
If I could just sit with You a while, I need You to hold me
Moment by moment, 'till forever passes by

When I know I've sinned when I should have been
Crying out my God and hidden in you
Lord I need you now, more than I know how
So I humbly bow, hidden in you

If I could just sit with You a while, if You could just hold me
Nothing could touch me though I'm wounded, though I die
If I could just sit with You a while, I need You to hold me
Moment by moment, 'till forever passes by

If I could just sit with You a while, I need You to hold me
Moment by moment, 'till forever passes by

Moment by moment, 'till forever passes by

There is perhaps only one answer to why God has allowed "bad things" to happen, and I encourage you to stand on this truth in your darkest moments: *All things work together for good to them that love God, to them who are called according to His purpose (Romans 8:28).*

That word says "all things," which means what happened to you.

A Practical Way to Walk Out Forgiveness

In your journal, write down:

Whom do I need to forgive?

Do I need to include myself?

What do I need to forgive them or myself for?

Then meet with Jesus at the cross, and with the gift of His grace, choose to forgive anyone who has hurt you and you know you have not forgiven. Ask the Holy Spirit to show you any unforgiveness you may be harboring unconsciously.

Meet with Jesus and the person who has hurt you at the foot of the cross. With God's grace, offer forgiveness to that person. Therefore, in the presence of Christ, say: "I forgive you, _____ (filling in the blank)."

The cross is also a grace place where you can go to seek forgiveness for what you have done. "Please forgive me for _____ (filling in the blank)."

It is essential to note here: forgiveness and trust are very separate issues. Where trust has been broken, it has to be restored to continue to do relationship with that individual. Therefore, you can forgive and still not choose to have relationship when trust has not been restored. You can also forgive, though the other may not acknowledge his or her wrong.

Forgiveness Model

As I said earlier, to not forgive can be pictured as not letting someone off the hook or making yourself their judge and jury. They become accountable to you for their injustices versus being accountable to God. Another picture of unforgiveness is putting in prison those you refuse to forgive. What you may not realize though is that your choice to withhold forgiveness automatically puts you in prison, too. The only difference is that you hold the key to setting both of you free by choosing to forgive. God has made provision for forgiveness by the blood of Christ. He gives you grace to forgive those that have caused your pain and deep hurt. To choose not to forgive those who have hurt you will bind you to the hurt and person who injured you. Thus you become captive. Abba God means to set you free, no matter how grave the injury. He is the Restorer, Repairer, and Redeemer.

Make a habit of forgiveness. "Keep short accounts," the old saints used to say—do not store up hurts. Keep no record of wrongs. Forgiveness is also an ongoing process. When the hurts have been particularly deep or the bitterness held for a long time, you may need to forgive the one who hurt you more than once. When the old angry or sad thoughts come up about what that person did to you, go back to the cross and forgive them again.

Use the practical way to forgive from page 53. When you have completed the forgiveness process, hear God's words to you, "You are forgiven."

FORGIVENESS MODEL

When we do not forgive, we place another on a hook.
We become their judge and we decide when they are acceptable enough to be let off the hook

When we do not forgive, we place another in prison. At the same time, we sentence ourselves. The only difference is, we hold the KEY- Forgiveness!

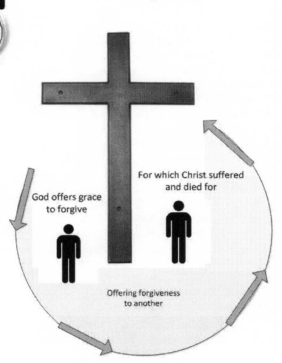

For which Christ suffered and died for

God offers grace to forgive

Offering forgiveness to another

Roselene Coblentz, Ph.D, LMFT

Your Daily Habit of Forgiveness

Develop a daily habit of forgiveness. From your sit place, forgive others and yourself with the grace of God and live daily in the truth, "I am forgiven."

Blaine's Story

Returning from a weekend men's retreat, Blaine shared with his friend Stan memories of his childhood story, "My parents were more interested in partying with their friends and using alcohol and drugs than caring for me and my sister." Blaine shared how his mom had bought him an old, beat-up guitar at a garage sale to get him to stop begging for one. It had become his solace with all the chaos of yelling and fighting between his parents. Blaine didn't say it out loud, but he remembered his dad throwing him out the back door at age eight when he was drunk. He continued to share with his buddy, "Even as an adult my parents choose not to engage with me. It hurts a lot that my life doesn't matter to them. My mom favors my brother and sister over me and doesn't show much interest in my wife or her granddaughter. It makes me feel really sad." After a time of silence between them, Blaine continued, "Then there is my dad, who rarely checks in on me, even just to ask how I am doing. He is not much different than when I was growing up. He is still self-focused. I can't remember a time that he affirmed, encouraged, or spent time with me."

At the men's retreat, Blaine had been challenged to look at his childhood story to see who he needed to forgive and for what he needed to forgive them. They also had been encouraged to bless those that had wounded them. He understood that blessing others was not the same as having a trusted relationship with them. That was not a possibility for his parents did not reflect trustworthiness to him. It was a new thought to him, however, to not only forgive, but bless his parents. He knew it was important for his healing to forgive his parents for their neglect, abuse, favoritism, loss of affirmation, and acceptance. After his forgiveness prayer, he asked God to bless his parents with God's love, grace, wisdom, favor, and protection. He experienced a peace he had never felt before.

Finally, R. T. Kendall, in his book *Total Forgiveness*, says forgiveness is not complete until we can bless our "enemies." So the last and most powerful step of your forgiveness journey is to ask God to bless the one who has wounded you. Great grace will be yours in return.

Personal Growth Questions

1. List your present, "uncensored" beliefs about forgiveness, not what your head knows to be true, but what you really believe in your heart or what your behaviors reveal to you. Which ones need to be replaced with truth?

2. What experience have you had with unforgiveness in your own life?

3. Who do you need to forgive and what do you need to forgive them for?

4. Take the journey to the cross to forgive that person. Write down in your journal what happened during that journey.

5. What does it mean to you to "keep short accounts" with one another, in terms of keeping no record of wrongs?

Prayer

God, I worship You for You are merciful and compassionate, God. It is by the blood of Jesus that all my sins are forgiven. With Your grace, I can forgive those that have sinned against me. I can forgive me. Show me mercy and unfailing love in erasing all my sin, purifying, and washing me clean for then I am whiter than snow. All this is because of the blood shed by Jesus at the cross. The blood covers me. My broken, repentant heart is all I have to offer. I come humbly before You to receive mercy for all my sins. I come to the cross and with Your grace, I choose to forgive all those that have hurt me. I trust You to help me to always forgive others. Your grace is sufficient to help me forgive myself. And then God, I desire that You bless those that have hurt me with Your mercy, love, and grace. Mark my life with forgiveness as only You can by the blood of Jesus. In Jesus Name, Amen. (Psalms 51:1-2, 4, 7, 17 NLT)

Resources

Embracing the Love of God, James Bryan Smith
The Five Languages of Apology, Gary Chapman, Jennifer Thomas
Total Forgiveness, R. T. Kendall

Notes...

Week Six: Your Healing Plan

I trust that from your "sit place with God:" you are practicing being more attentive to your everyday thoughts, experiencing grace, aligning your will with His grace in your daily choices, and offering forgiveness as needed. This is a journey of intimacy with God as you travel through each day's situations, sharing with Him all that concerns you. Be patient with yourself and keep pursuing Him as you work on integrating each of these understandings into your life.

This week you will begin to create your healing plan, preparing yourself for any life situation that causes deep pain and disappointment.

Consider this: there is great value in having a financial, health, or retirement plan to be prepared for the future. Most of us also want to be prepared for any unforeseen crisis that could occur, such as a job loss or serious health challenge. What we don't prepare for in advance are the inevitable and sometimes devastating hurts and disappointments we will face during our lives. We tend, rather, to ignore the hurt and the pain and continue down the road or we get stuck in our emotions—neither response cares for the wound well. Thus, perhaps we can agree that a healing plan would be a great strategy for our personal lives to care for each of us daily or when any challenge enters into our world unexpectedly.

God of All Comfort

Your hurts need the healing presence of Jesus. Last week, we saw that God is a God of mercy, Who has forgiven all our sins, restored us to fellowship with Himself, and surrounded us with His favor through the sacrifice of His Son. This same merciful God comes to you to as the God of all Comfort as expressed in the Scriptures: *Praise be to the God and Father of our Lord Jesus Christ, the Father of compassion and the God of all comfort, who comforts us in all our troubles (2 Corinthians 1:3-4, NIV).*

He first comes to offer you more grace to bring the comfort and compassion you need for your pain and deep hurts. When you share your hurts with Him, you will experience His attentiveness, affection, care, and comfort as He is present to you. Then you will listen to His healing words regarding your personal wounds and losses. His personal words will always match the Word of God and the principles of His Word. Though the difficult life experiences remain a part of your history, when you revisit them you will experience His healing presence of love and His personal words to you. "You will have a new way of remembering" your story, as the movie *Saving Mr. Banks* expressed. This time Jesus is present in your story, healing you as only He can.

Remember, this is a process. Healing your heart is a journey, not an overnight stay. Be faithful to the journey and stay as long as needed to receive the fullness of His healing. To revisit the sites of your injuries is often frightening; therefore, most do not choose to return there. This is understandable. But you must remember, you do not return there alone, as you may have experienced initially; now the Presence of Jesus returns with you. As you stop, listen to His kind, gentle voice, and with His strong, loving arms around you, He will heal your heart.

Carrie's Story

Carrie struggled with her choices in college that led to her decision to have an abortion. She couldn't imagine being able to care for a child and continue college, much less work full-time. For her, it was her only option to stay on track with her life as she understood it. Now five years later, married and having given birth to her son, her abortion began to torment her. Having experienced giving birth, Carrie changed her view on abortion. Sleep deprivation and her ever-present self-defeating thoughts began to pull her even deeper into the dark realm of depression. Finally, she sought wise counsel with a therapist who helped her to exchange her self-defeating thoughts for truthful thoughts, decreasing her depression. Carrie began to make good on the grace of God, believing and receiving His Perfect Love, regardless of the abortion. She received forgiveness, and at the cross with Christ present, she received forgiveness for herself. She let herself off the hook and released herself from prison. Depression gradually relinquished its strong hold on her.

Carrie, with the help of her therapist, now embraces God's comfort from her "sit place with Abba God," where she visualizes her last vacation in the gardens at Glorietta, New Mexico. She welcomes the Presence of Jesus to sit with her. Visualizing His strong, loving arms around her, tears streaming down her face, she shares all her tormenting thoughts and deep pain: "I am so sorry for taking another life. Please forgive me. Help me to forgive myself." Carrie listens to His voice, His thoughts highlighted to her: "You are deeply loved, you are forgiven, there is no rejection or judgment, only My grace and acceptance to you." She holds tightly to these two truths as she watches with the eyes of her heart, Abba God, opening up that dark wound, making a way for the pain to be released and extracted. Carrie observes the healing oil being poured in, all the while being held in His strong, loving arms.

She shares with her therapist, "I always feared I would be judged, rejected, and shamed by God; instead I experienced His acceptance, mercy, forgiveness, and love. I could never have imagined this would be a part of my story. I am so grateful Jesus visited me in my story." Then for her eyes only, she saw her child in the arms of God being loved by Him, smiling at her. For so long she had remembered her story with pain and shame; now she could remember it with God's healing presence, a new way of remembering. Carrie needed this healing to enjoy her marriage fully and love her newborn son with all her heart. She knew one day she would be able to share her story, her Jesus story.

Two Lies

Our culture is defined by two fundamental beliefs: the choices I make impact only me, and my needs are the only ones that matter. These beliefs are untrue. What hurts you often hurts many others. You are ruled by unseen forces that work through your selfishness and emotions, marring your life and the lives around you with deep wounds that often have life-long effects. I have yet to meet one person who has not been wounded by another's selfishness and wounded emotional state. I also believe that none of us would say we have not wounded another in our selfishness and emotional responses. Therefore, freedom is for what has happened to you and the choices you have made that have harmed yourself and others.

• • •

Healed Hurt Model

The first step is to visualize your safe, loved place with Abba God, your "sit place." If you can go to your physical "sit place," you can invite Him there as well. Secondly, invite the Presence of Jesus to sit with you. Take a moment to wait for Him to come as your heart understands He is present to you. Don't rush. Be patient. When you believe He is present, continue to the next step. Third, share with Him your deep hurt from your story. Take the time to write in your journal about your hurt. Leave nothing out. Everything matters to God. He will listen as you pour out your heart to Him. You can trust Him to show care and comfort to you personally, as David expressed: *Trust in him at all times, you people; pour out your hearts to him, for God is our refuge (Psalm 62:8, NIV).* Paul in 2 Corinthians 1:3-5 (NKJV) agrees with David: *Praise be to the God and Father of our Lord Jesus Christ, the Father of compassion and the God of all comfort, who comforts us in all our troubles.*

His care and comfort can extract the pain from every wound. Sharing your hurt and receiving His care is a vital part to healing your heart. Fourth, as Abba God listens to you, pause, listening to His healing words to you. Begin writing the encouraging words He wants to share with you. His healing words will deliver you from your fears, heal your hurts, remove your shame, and give to you a radiance of joy and peace. You see Him and hear Him through the thoughts and pictures that come to your mind as you pray and listen to your heart. Sometimes we don't trust what we hear or see, but you can trust Abba God to respond to you in a way you can understand. Fifth, it is imperative that you receive and believe what He speaks to you personally. This will secure His healing work in you for a lifetime.

David confirms God's desire to heal your hurts when he says in Psalm 34:4-5, 15, 17-18 (NKJV*): I sought the Lord, and he answered me; he delivered me from all my fears. Those who look to him are radiant; their faces are never covered with shame. The eyes of the Lord are on the righteous and his ears are attentive to their cry; the righteous cry out, and the Lord hears them; he delivers them from all their troubles. The Lord is close to the brokenhearted and saves those who are crushed in spirit.*

From my own experience of dealing with past and present hurts, I know it is never comfortable or easy. Inviting the Presence of Jesus into your story and experiencing His healing presence and words is a worthy pursuit. It makes way for deep, satisfying, fulfilling relationships and a purposeful, promising destiny.

* * *

HEALED HURTS MODEL
Abba God comes with Grace to heal the hurts

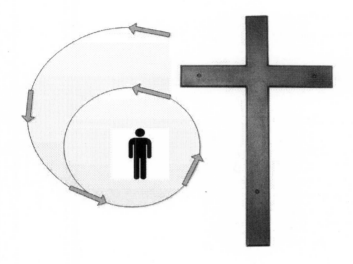

Roselene Coblentz, Ph.D, LMFT

Your Daily Habit of Healed Hurts

Develop a daily habit of healed hurts. From your sit place, share your hurts with God, listening and receiving His comfort and compassion and healing words of truth. He will teach you a new way of remembering your story, a Jesus story.

You alone cannot heal the hurt and its impact on your life or the lives of others; you need the help of God the Redeemer. Again, you must experience and practice within yourself the healing, help, and hope first before you can be truly effective in bringing lasting healing and change to others. God promises in His Word that He comes to restore you. Here is what He says, *And the God of all grace, who called you to his eternal glory in Christ, after you have suffered a little while, will himself restore you and make you strong, firm and steadfast (1 Peter 5:10, NIV).*

It Feels Like Redemption
By Michael English

I know how hopeless feels
When you're staring at the bottom of an empty hole
In my life I know how forgotten feels
Wondering if the world even knows who you are

But I've never known anything, felt anything
Like the love of Jesus
And it's hard to describe what's happening inside
But right now all I know is

It feels like redemption raining down on me
It feels like forgiveness is come to set me free
All my chains have been lifted
'Cause when the hands of love touch a broken life
It feels like redemption

Now I know how thankful feels
'Cause I am overwhelmed by this gift of grace
And I know how healing feels
'Cause all my pain and all my shame
And all my tears have been erased

It feels like redemption raining down on me
It feels like forgiveness is come to set me free
All my chains have been lifted
'Cause when the hands of love touch a broken life
It feels like

Say goodbye, the past is ending
Say hello to a new beginning
No more night
The sun is shining

Feels like redemption raining down on me
It feels like forgiveness is come to set me free
All my chains have been lifted
'Cause when the hands of love touch a broken life
And when the hands of love touch a broken life
It feels like redemption

I cried out to the Lord, He heard my cry
He healed my heart and He touched my life
It feels like redemption

So say goodbye, the past is ending
Say hello to a new beginning
Feels like
Feels like redemption
Retrieved from http://www.metrolyrics.com/feels-like-redemption-lyrics-michael-english.html

• • •

Personal Growth Questions

1. What is your greatest fear about revisiting your wounded places? What are the truths you need to substitute for that fear?

2. Ask the Lord to highlight one incident from your life when you were wounded and still need healing today. It may be something traumatic, or maybe something you have told yourself is "no big deal." Let the Lord bring it to your mind.

3. In your sit place with Abba God, visualize Him sitting down with you, listening very attentively to everything you are telling him about what happened to you in the incident above and what you felt. Then wait expectantly for His healing words or pictures.

4. Journal your experience with God, what He said to you or showed you, and how you feel now about the wound you shared with Him.

5. If you feel able, please share your story with your study group.

Prayer

My God, You are my God, my One and Only God. I seek You. I come to You. I need You. You will answer me and heal me of all my pain and disappointments. You are my Redeemer. I know that when I look to You, where my face is covered in shame and hurt; one look into Your face, my face will shine with Your radiant grace. You are attentive to all my prayers. I know You will hear, listen, and answer me. You are my Refuge. As the God of all Grace, You will journey with me in my difficult times. You as the Restorer-Redeemer will make me strong, steady, sure, and secure in Christ. From my sit place, You will show me affection with Your strong-loving arms wrapped around me as You care for my heart, mending it in the ways it needs Your healing grace. You will come close to heal my broken heart. Mark my life, my heart with healing, as the God of all Grace. (Psalm 34:4-5, 15, 17-18)

Resources

Changes that Heal, Dr. Henry Cloud
Healing is a Choice, Stephen Arterburn
For Women: Fierce Beauty, Kim Meeder
Captivating, John & Staci Eldredge
Mended, Angie Smith
For Men: Healing of the Masculine Soul, Gordon Dalbey
Wild at Heart, John Eldredge

Notes...

Week Seven: Your Grief Journey

Grief on your intimacy journey with God is your focus this week. Grief comes into all of our lives, but is often not acknowledged or healed because there are greater demands on our time or the process seems too painful. But to do life well, you must pause as often and as long as you need to, to care for your grief.

I want to begin by sharing a few important facts about grief, present to you several visuals that will be beneficial to understanding grief, and lastly, suggest a way to grieve your losses effectively and continue your life journey with God's comfort and compassion.

Grief is the emotional response to loss. Loss is more easily understood to be the result of death or divorce, but there are many other losses as well: the loss of friendship, the loss of childhood, the loss of trust in marriage, loss of jobs, as well as the loss of hope through unfulfilled personal desires. Where there is hurt, there is loss, and this loss must be acknowledged and grieved.

Recovery from grief may appear beyond your capacity to manage, yet God reminds us that He is here to help and will restore your heart. As David writes in the 23rd Psalm, *He restores my soul* (NKJV) (And David certainly experienced many losses!). Though society often fails to create a space to grieve, time to grieve well is crucial. Today, a grieving individual may be given three days off, and then after six months or maybe a year, the message is delivered: "You need to be over this. You need to get past this. You need

• • •

to be living your life as though no loss ever occurred." This is so not the case. Every person needs to be allowed to grieve at their own pace and in their own way. And I might add: never on their own or alone.

Two Visual Pictures of Grief

Grieving has sometimes been compared to driving a car. When grief has occurred it is important to look forward through the windshield, to continue as best as you can to do life forward functionally. At the same time, you must pay attention to the rear view mirror, looking backwards to feel those emotions your loss has generated and address the challenges you face as a result of your loss. So often we choose one or the other: living forward as though no loss occurred or backwards, getting stuck in our feelings, neglecting our present, daily responsibilities. To grieve well, it is important to do both simultaneously, living life moving forward as your present responsibilities demand and looking backward to care for your loss. Of course, grief is not a straightforward process; sometimes we are only able to "do" forward and sometimes we are better able to look back. The important point is to not get stuck in one or the other.

The most important way to grieve well is from your "sit place with God." As challenging as it may be to identify your feelings, you must be present to them, and give them permission to exist, without judgment or without acting on them. *Just be with them.* Invite the God of all comfort to "sit with you," bringing you the comfort and compassion you need to feel these emotions. As you feel your emotions, you can begin let go of the negative thoughts or painful images attached to them, dropping them into the stream of God's love, where He will take them out to sea. You can then hold on to the good of your memories to be remembered always.

Remember, this a journey; take the time needed. Gradually, the Presence of Jesus will keep you moving forward, and He also will help you pause when you need to reflect on your sadness. Gradually, joy will join your sadness as you are able to hold on to your valued memories. David reminds you of this truth, *Weeping may endure for a night, but joy comes in the morning (Psalms 30:5, NKJV).*

Here is another grief picture: the emotions of grief are often experienced like waves. Waves come to shore as they please, with their own intensity and frequency. Waves also recede out to sea. Like these waves, grief emotions have their own flow in and out and their own intensity. By the way, waves do not take into consideration that you are at work, at the grocery store, in a meeting, or caring for any other daily responsibility. They just come! It is important that you remember: God is aware of and caring for your every emotion. He will come with each wave and be your Comfort, Refuge, and Strength. *Blessed be the God and Father of our Lord Jesus Christ, the Father of mercies and God of all Comfort (2 Corinthians 1:3, NKJV).* Remember to care for each wave of emotion from your "sit place with God." Be intentional in sitting with God and if you are able, writing in your journal your thoughts and feelings.

Each wave of emotion may be joined by thoughts and images that need to be let go. Releasing negative thoughts and images connected to your loss will allow you to continue your journey. It is important that you make good on the grace of God to let go of every negative thought and behavior that may be connected to anger, guilt, or regret. Here are a few examples: *"I should have called," "I shouldn't have said that," "I didn't say I love you enough" "I was only thinking of myself when I...,"* as well as angry gestures you may have made.

Anger in the Grief Process

Anger is an emotion that often shows its face on the grief journey. I encourage you to give it your attention. Feel it without judging or reacting to it. Take note what thoughts or images are connected to it. You can write these down in your journal. Then drop each one of these thoughts or mental pictures into the stream of God's love. If you find that you are angry with God, share your feelings with Him. He can handle it. There is no judgment or condemnation from God for your feelings of anger. Blaming God is often present in losses. It is true He is in control of all things, but remember as well that He has created you and everyone else with a free will to make wise choices. Where grief has come because of someone's wrongful use of free will, offering forgiveness to him or her is a part of your grief journey. With the grace of God, forgive them for each way that their choice has wounded you. Then receive God's healing for your grief.

Self-blame is another obstacle often encountered on the grief journey. What did I do wrong to cause this to happen? I must not have had enough faith or she would have been healed. There must be something wrong with me. These thoughts must be taken to God in your sit place. Allow Him to speak truth to you, speak comfort to you, and take these thoughts away from you. It is also important to take yourself off the hook; if you need to, forgive yourself, as we discussed in week five.

Finally, there are many questions we do not know the answer to—*why did God allow my husband to develop cancer? Why didn't he heal him? Why did God allow my daughter to be killed in a car accident? Where was God when my father was molesting me*? We live in a fallen world, where terrible things happen. There is no easy answer as to why God seems to allow hurt and suffering. But in the end we must come back to the foundational truth that God loves us with an everlasting love. And that *He will work all things to the good for those who love Him (Romans 8:28)*. Hang on to that truth. Come to Him and let Him show His comfort and compassion to you. Once your anger has been experienced and overcome with His grace and mercy, it will open the way for more sadness to emerge to continue the healing journey.

Letting go of that which is holding you back or keeping you stuck in pain will help you move forward on your grief journey. Gradually, you will welcome the joy that comes from remembering the good memories. Take note, if there are no good memories to hold on to, it will be vital to remember that you can hold on to God. He is always with you, He never leaves you, He is good, and He loves you. He will give you hope, comfort, and strength. There is your joy! Hold on to His healing, true words to you.

This joy does not overcome your sadness; it only comes to care for you in your sadness. In due season, joy steps in front of sadness, but can never remove all the sadness of your loss. I believe grief is often a lifetime journey, depending on what your loss is. Sadness may always be present, but joy will carry you alongside your sadness throughout your life. Your intimacy with God, sharing with Him all your thoughts and feelings, will always help you in your time of need. These are His truthful words to you: *You will grieve, but your grief will turn to joy (John 16:20, NKJV)*.

John's Story

John struggled daily just going to work for months after the loss of his young adult son to suicide. Some days he just sat in the dark with his Bible, trusting that God would strengthen him from the waves crashing upon his soul. One day he shared with his brother, "Without God's help the waves would pull me in and under for good. Some days, I think I am going under. But He keeps me coming up for air with a tiny bit of hope that I may survive this most devastating storm of my life."

John often has to disentangle anger from sadness. He thinks of all the things he should have done that could have prevented this awful thing from happening. After feeling his anger, often in crashing waves, John begins to drop the "should's" into the stream of God's love, feeling his deep sadness, but also trusting the God of all comfort to come and sit with him.

John continues to share with his brother, "I think of my son every day--what I want to share with him and all the adventures we could have experienced together." Letting his tears flow, he continues, "I want to ask his forgiveness for not listening to him, not understanding him, or spending enough time with him." Silence filled the room where John and his brother were. Only sadness was present to them. John knew it was okay to sit with this sadness. He knew that one day he would also let go of self-judgment and self-blame. In time, he would welcome joy on the journey, remembering the shared times of camping, fishing, rock climbing, and all the movies he and his son enjoyed together.

> What we have once enjoyed deeply we can never lose. All that we love deeply becomes a part of us.
> Helen Keller

> The risk of love is loss, and the price of loss is grief - But the pain of grief is only a shadow when compared with the pain of never risking love.
> Hilary Stanton Zunin

> There is a sacredness in tears. They are not the mark of weakness, but of power. They speak more eloquently than ten thousand tongues. They are the messengers of overwhelming grief, of deep contrition, and of unspeakable love.
> Washington Irving

Grief Model

Mountains. Here is another way to process your grief when it requires life changes. List your loss. If due to your loss, you are now challenged with loneliness, regret, financial distress, single parenting, anxiety, selling your home, moving, or sleep-deprivation, to name just a few, each one of them can seem like a mountain to climb. Label the mountains you need to climb and work through. It is also true that facing each mountain calls for different emotions from you. It is necessary to climb each mountain separately and care for the particular emotions as you integrate into your new life.

Isaiah encourages your heart with these words: *So do not fear, for I am with you; do not be dismayed, for I am your God. I will strengthen you and help you; I will uphold you with my righteous right hand (Isaiah 41:10, NIV).* List what your new life will look like when you have climbed to the top of the mountain.

As you integrate into your new life take His help and the help of others to work through the loneliness, create a new financial plan, seek effective ways to manage single parenting, find the help needed to lower your anxiety, or get more quality sleep. Facing each of these mountains will help to rebuild your new life apart from your loss. It is never easy, but with God and others coming alongside, you can journey through your grief and step into your new life.

Waves. It is very useful to process these grief waves with your journal. From your sit place, write about your **feelings** connected to the present grief wave. Secondly, if there are any negative feelings or images, **let go** of them, like dropping them in the stream of God. Third, write what you choose to **hold on** to your memories and/or healing words of God.

GRIEF MODEL

LOSS	MOUNTAINS	INTEGRATE INTO NEW LIFE

Grief Waves

1. **Feel** the emotion experienced with each wave:_____
2. **Let go of** thoughts/images connected to wave (after Abba God has brought healing to you) into the stream of God
3. **Hold on** to God's healing words to you and your memories.

Strobe, M.S, Schut,H Dual Process Model
Roselene Coblentz, Ph.D, LMFT

Your Daily Habit of Grief

Develop a daily habit of grief. From your sit place, grieve well your losses. The God of Comfort will care for your sadness. As you continue your grief journey make a place for joy to sit beside sadness.

A Word to Those in Relationship with Someone on a Grieving Journey

Offer comfort in the form of a hug if the person is open to it. Speak words such as, "I am very sorry this has happened to you." Just sit with them and listen to them. Do not offer solutions. Do not say, "I understand what you are feeling," if you have not felt this loss yourself. There are many variables to each loss. Do not ask, "What can I do for you?" They are feeling overwhelmed and may not be able to put their finger on what they need. Be sensitive, attentive, and observant of what their needs are. Call them, invite them for lunch, or ask what errands you could do for them. Be mindful of important dates and holidays or events on their grief journey: birthday, anniversary, date of death, child's birth date, or special occasions. Ask them what dates or memorable events are important to them. Then write them down to remember them on those dates. Check in often. Not just for a few weeks, or several months, but in some cases several years or a lifetime depending on the loss.

Remember: every person will grieve differently; there is no universal timetable or formula. Journaling can be very helpful in processing your grief. In God's Presence, you can write down—or shout out!--your uncensored thoughts and feelings. Then wait to hear His comforting words to you. Write these words in your journal, too, so that you begin to build a record of God's grace and comfort to you. You can return to that record when you feel the waves washing over you.

Gracie's Story

Gracie's story involves much grieving, one being the loss of her childhood. Healthy childhood experiences build trust; they teach you to receive and give love; they lay a foundation for self-acceptance and a sense of self-worth. Gracie tells her dear friend, "None of these was present to carry me from childhood to adulthood. My story has many broken pieces of molestation, rape, physical and verbal abuse. Emotional nurture was absent from my home. I experienced deep loneliness. There was no place that was safe and secure. Fear and rage surrounded me day and night. However, I believe Abba God gave me a personal word from Psalm 16 at age eight that was and still is my stronghold: *You will make known to me the path of life; you will fill me with joy in your presence, with eternal treasures at your right hand (Psalm 16:11, NIV).*

It was this word, "you will show me the path of life" that has helped Gracie to grieve her losses and climb every mountain as she walks into her adult years. Her mountains have included: distrust, insecurity, a sense of being unworthy, feeling unloved, anger, hopelessness, rejection, shame, and fear. But Gracie slowly learned to trust God, herself, and trustworthy friends. She completed her education and now is involved in teaching and mentoring women. God has indeed worked "all things for the good" in her life.

Gracie has been diligent to believe at the core of her being the truth that she is deeply loved and accepted by God. With His help and strength, she has learned to care for every wave of sadness in her "sit place with God," to release all her angry thoughts and painful memories into the stream of God's love, and to hold on to His grace and loving kindness daily. She also has been diligent to take hold of God's grace to forgive those who hurt her. In the years of grieving and facing challenges, Gracie has invited joy to come alongside her sadness. Today, her life does not reflect her losses, but God's healing grace. Therefore, as she shares with her friend, "My heart's desire is always, as Paul says, *To finish the race and complete the task the Lord Jesus has given me—the task of testifying to the good news of God's grace with my life" (Acts 20:24, NIV).*

The Importance of Thanksgiving

In the midst of loss and grief, thanking God and praising God seems counter-intuitive, but this action and attitude of the heart is vital for your healing. Paul says, *Rejoice always, pray without ceasing, in everything give thanks; for this is the will of God in Christ Jesus for you (I Thessalonians 5:16-18, NKJV).* You are not thanking God for the loss, for what happened to you, but you are thanking Him for Who He is. For all that He has done for you. And for all that He will do for you in your future. Giving thanks when your world is turned upside down is no easy task, but it will strengthen you when everything seems impossible or overwhelming.

In your sit place, make a thanksgiving list: enumerate 10 things God has done for you and then express your thanks to Him for each of these blessings. Maybe these include: saving you, providing for you when you lost your job, for giving you a devoted spouse, maybe simply for the strength to get out of bed, to go to work, to take care of your children, for friends that call, or for God's presence, and His promise to be with you in your darkest of days. Remembering how God has helped you will renew your hope and faith. Continue to practice daily Paul's words to rejoice, pray, and give thanks while you continue on your grief journey.

* * *

Personal Growth Questions

1. Identify a significant loss in your life. Describe how you dealt with the emotions of that loss.

2. What was your greatest challenge in grieving that loss?

3. What are your greatest fears or challenges to just sit with the sadness of your losses?

4. Describe a loss you feel you may not have grieved fully or effectively. What can you do now to grieve that loss?

5. What was the most significant truth you learned from this week's study regarding loss and grief? What would you put on your thanksgiving list (p. 77) during your season of grief?

Prayer

God, I praise You for being the Father of Compassion and the God of all Comfort. You will comfort me as I pour out my sadness to You. You are my Refuge. God, you are my Shepherd, my Good Shepherd. You provide for me everything I need. You withhold no good thing from me. You are my Provider. You bring me to Your green pastures. It is here that You will feed me, nourish, and nurture me. You lead me to Your still, quiet waters. Your Word will refresh, strengthen, and sustain me when I am weary, overwhelmed, and exhausted. You will sit with me to restore my soul, my spirit, mind, and emotions. God, you desire to prosper me in my soul and body. You will show me Your care and comfort. Mark me with Your personal care and comfort me as You are the God of all Comfort. In Jesus Name, Amen. (2 Corinthians 1:3-4; Psalm 23:1-3; III John 1:2)

* * *

Resources

A Grace Disguised, Jerry Sittser (any loss)
When Grief Comes, Kirk H. Neely (death-general)
The Power of Praise and Worship, Terry Law (death and divorce)
I Will Carry You, Angie Smith (miscarriages)
Silent Grief, Clara Hinton (miscarriages)
Moving Forward After Divorce, David Frisbie
Champagne for the Soul, Mike Mason (joy in times of sadness)
Aftershock, David Cox and Candy Arrington (suicide)

Notes...

Week Eight: Your Journey OUT of Darkness

In Week Eight and Week Nine, I will share on the subject of spiritual influences of darkness and light. There are many excellent books written on these topics and how they operate and influence your life. I encourage you to read them to further your understanding. For this week, my primary purpose is to help you understand the role of darkness in undermining everything in your life.

The greatest challenge for you is your unawareness or denial of this presence of darkness and your lack of strategy to deal with Satan's plans to create havoc on your life and the lives of others around you. It is important to understand that there is a real, live battle between God and the forces of darkness for your life. Peter communicates this in *I Peter 5:8: ...Your enemy the devil prowls around like a roaring lion looking for someone to devour (NIV.)* In your "sit place with Abba God," give Him permission to teach you and give you understanding of the way Satan influences you in your past and present hurts, disappointments, desires, attitudes, thoughts, emotions, choices, and relationships.

I define "darkness" as everything associated with Satan, such as hate, fear, lies, destruction, and judgment; everything that destroys the life of God in His loved people. It is so important for you to be aware of the enemy's strategies to kill, steal, and destroy the life of God in you as John states, *The thief comes only to steal and kill and destroy...(John 10:10, NIV).* To be blind to this truth is to leave yourself open and vulnerable to the enemy's tactics.

• • •

Satan's Attack on Your Thoughts

Before you get started I want you to give attention to thoughts and their role as the primary tactic of the enemy. One very important piece of information that I believe Satan wants to downplay is your thought life. This creates the most critical problem for humanity. The first place you see where thoughts play a role in Scriptures is in the very first book of the Bible. It is in the Garden of Eden with Satan having a conversation with Eve. *Now the serpent was more cunning than any beast of the field which the LORD God had made. And he said to the woman, "Has God indeed said, 'You shall not eat of every tree of the garden'?" And the woman said to the serpent, "We may eat the fruit of the trees of the garden; but of the fruit of the tree which is in the midst of the garden, God has said, 'You shall not eat it, nor shall you touch it, lest you die. Then the serpent said to the woman, "You will not surely die. For God knows that in the day you eat of it your eyes will be opened, and you will be like God, knowing good and evil." So when the woman saw that the tree was good for food, that it was pleasant to the eyes, and a tree desirable to make one wise, she took of its fruit and ate. She also gave to her husband with her, and he ate (Genesis 3:1-6, NKJV).*

You can see very quickly Eve's thoughts and how they are being influenced by Satan. She begins to question and doubt what has been her truth from God. This is why Paul encourages believers to take captive every thought, *...bringing every thought into captivity to the obedience of Christ (II Corinthians 10:5, NKJV)* and to renew your mind, *....be transformed by the renewing of your mind, that you may prove what is that good and acceptable and perfect will of God (Romans 12:2, NKJV)*. Satan's first strategy is your thought life.

Your thought life matters, and it is important that as you learned in Week Three, your thoughts match the thoughts of God. Too often we neglect to address our thoughts, leaving them open to the influence of Satan and the forces of darkness. Remember Satan is known as the father of lies: *When he lies, he speaks his native language, for he is a liar and the father of lies (John 8:44, NIV)*. The opposite is said of God: *It is impossible for God to lie... (Hebrews 6:18, NIV)*.

Take note of the wisdom from the book of Proverbs, *For as he thinks in his heart, so is he... (Proverbs 23:7, NKJV)*. Out of your thoughts and beliefs, thought patterns are developed leading to your behavioral choices, which then impact your relationships. There is no action taken, negative or positive,

● ● ●

without being first connected to a thought. Here is your problem, as well as the problem of all mankind.

With this understanding, I want to bring you to another important truth. Paul states *Who has known the mind of the LORD that he may instruct Him? But we have the mind of Christ (I Corinthians 2:16, NKJV).* This is very important to remember daily as you journey through life: draw from the thoughts of God, to remain under the influence of Light and Truth. I will address more on the thoughts of God in week nine.

Strategy to Resist Satan

Having introduced you to the power of your thoughts and Satan's plan to kill, steal, and destroy the life of God in you, I want to give you a strategy that works and is simple in form, but not necessarily easy to walk out in your humanness. Therefore, you will need to utilize the truth of Week Four, "to make good on the grace of God to walk out."

Let us look at your role and response and God's role and response in this spiritual battle as beautifully portrayed in Psalm 18.

1. Our worship to God
2. Our call for help
3. God declares war as Mighty Warrior
4. God's warring response to rescue you

Your Worship to God

First, your worship, praise, and delight in the Lord is strategic. No matter your situation, always first enter into your "sit place with Abba God" to worship Him for His nature and character, and in humble adoration of Him, praise Him who created you and loves you with His life and heart. In all your circumstances, worship and praise Him with everything within you as expressed by David: *I love you, Lord, my strength. The Lord is my rock, my fortress and my deliverer; my God is my rock, in whom I take refuge, my shield and the horn of my salvation, my stronghold (Ps. 18:2.).* God delights in your worship as you honor Him. You can see the value of your thoughts in worship, praise, adoration, and exhortation of God. These will bring light, life, and peace when struggling in your difficult, dark times. David shares an example of how true thoughts, God thoughts, are like light: *Your word is a lamp to my feet, And a light to my path (Psalms 119:11, 105 NKJV).* Paul agrees with David and encourages you as well to use your words to *Rejoice always, give thanks in all circumstances; for this is God's will for you in Christ Jesus (1 Thessalonians 5:16, 18, NIV).*

Your 911 Call

Second, God desires to hear your 911 calls, as I refer to them. He is waiting for them to act on your behalf. *I called to the Lord, who is worthy of praise, and I have been saved from my enemies. The cords of death entangled me; the torrents of destruction overwhelmed me. The cords of the grave coiled around me; the snares of death confronted me. In my distress I called to the Lord; I cried to my God for help. From his temple he heard my voice; my cry came before him, into his ear (Psalm 18:3-6, NIV).*

Don't delay; express your thoughts and feelings to him; all your fears, insecurities, and struggles. He desires to fight for you. Remember: it is one thing to share your thoughts and feelings with God; it is another thing to come into agreement with them. God desires to hear your thoughts and heart and what you would like Him to do on your behalf.

Vince's Story

A day after receiving his paycheck, Vince knew he was in trouble when he looked at his bank account. In his garage, he began to speak to God. "God, you are God, my One and Only true God. You will never leave me on my own or alone. You hear, listen, and answer me. I give thanks over and over again for how many times you have provided for me financially, while always reminding me to stop using drugs. I have listened to the enemy that I can't say no to drugs. I can't say no to the anxious feelings. I can't choose to believe truth and much less be free. I will be forever controlled by these thoughts and my drug usage.

"Here is my desperate cry. Help me break free once and for all from this drug addiction and the thoughts that are connected to them. Forgive me, God, for my addiction and the lies that are becoming an all-consuming god to me. Come, help me! I desire you to be my one and only God. I surrender my mind and choices to you. I choose to believe truthfully, I can with your help and strength experience freedom from this bondage."

God Declares War

Third, God desires to respond to your 911 call. He declares He is Mighty Warrior and greater is He than the enemy advancing towards you. Watch what He does when your call is patched through to Him.

God as Mighty Warrior declares war on the enemy on your behalf. As He hears your cries, Mighty Warrior parts the heavens and comes down, declaring war. The visual image of His warring presence on your behalf is nothing short of amazing! It is like an earthquake, a volcanic eruption, and a hail storm merging as one in His thundering declaration I AM GOD: there will be no other gods before me, and these children are MINE!

This is revealed to you by David in *Psalm 18:7-15*: *The earth trembled and quaked, and the foundations of the mountains shook; they trembled because he was angry. Smoke rose from his nostrils; consuming fire came from his mouth, burning coals blazed out of it. He parted the heavens and came down; dark clouds were under his feet. He mounted the cherubim and flew; he soared on the wings of the wind. He made darkness his covering, his canopy around him— the dark rain clouds of the sky. Out of the brightness of his presence clouds advanced, with hailstones and bolts of lightning. The Lord thundered from heaven; the voice of the Most High resounded. He shot his arrows and scattered the enemy, with great bolts of lightning he routed them. The valleys of the sea were exposed and the foundations of the earth laid bare at your rebuke, Lord, at the blast of breath from your nostrils.*

It is important for you to remind yourself that God fights for you, wars for you. In His eternal love for you He desires to help you live your life in permanent liberation. He is not interested in partially "set free," as John says. The picture David shares is also confirmed by Isaiah: *I will go before you and will level the mountains; I will break down gates of bronze and cut through bars of iron. I will give you hidden treasures, riches stored in secret places, so that you may know that I am the Lord, the God of Israel, who summons you by name (Isaiah 45:2, 3, NIV).* God is committed to your freedom from everything that challenges you. Hear His words, "I am Mighty Warrior. I am here to deliver and to fully rescue you because I delight in you." I will leave you with one thought: see the beauty and power of God's words and the freedom He wants to bring to your life. Only God's truthful words and thoughts have the power to do this. Lying thoughts bring death and destruction.

* * *

God's Rescue Plan

Fourth, your Mighty Warrior fulfills His rescue plan for you without a hitch. *He reached down from on high and took hold of me; he drew me out of deep waters. He rescued me from my powerful enemy, from my foes, who were too strong for me. They confronted me in the day of my disaster, but the Lord was my support. He brought me out into a spacious place; he rescued* me *because he delighted in me (Psalm 18:7-19, NIV).* This is a picture of God's heart toward you, as He wars on your behalf.

Psalm 18 reflects the God of Light/Mighty Warrior as He descends from heaven in response to your call for help and mercy from the one who comes to kill, steal, and destroy you. He expresses Himself *out of the brightness of his presence* (v.12) declaring His awesome power over the forces of evil and darkness for the purposes of *rescuing me from my powerful enemy who was too strong for me* (v. 17). He *delights in rescuing you* (v. 18). Psalm 18 is also confirmed in Colossians 2:15: *And having disarmed the powers and authorities, he made a public spectacle of them, triumphing over them by the cross.* The cross, the shed blood of Jesus is where your deliverance is rooted. This is where every spirit of darkness is destroyed, demolished, and extinguished.

Light of His Presence overcomes ALL darkness

His power triumphs over ALL evil

He delights in rescuing ALL His children

ALL influences of darkness disarmed by the cross

*"Now the Lord is the Spirit, and where the
Spirit of the Lord is, this is
(ALL) freedom."*

2 Corinthians 3:17, NIV

Melody's Story

Melody, a fourth grade teacher, can't imagine that God would war for her. Her thoughts and feelings of unworthiness are overwhelming; day and night she is tormented by them. No one has ever fought for her. Her father and ex-husband never made her a priority. Why would God? As she hears her own thought, "why would God," she believes the Holy Spirit is telling her that is not God's voice, but the voice of the enemy, and she is not to come into agreement with it. She pauses and reads her daily devotional, *Rejoice always, pray continually, give thanks in all circumstances; for this is God's will for you in Christ Jesus (1 Thessalonians 5:16-18, NIV). Trust in him at all times, you people; pour out your hearts to him, for God is our refuge (Psalm 62:8, NIV).* He *delights in rescuing you (Psalm18:18, NIV).*

Melody decides to take a chance that God will war and rescue her as no other has in her past. She prays the only prayer she can, but nonetheless, the very much needed one: "God, please come rescue me from unworthiness. My heart longs to be delighted in. Deliver me from this dark, harassing spirit of unworthiness. I choose with your help to send the spirit of unworthiness to the cross in Jesus' Name by the blood of the Lamb. I no longer choose to engage in unworthy thoughts, but your thoughts of worthiness. I embrace your rescue plan for me."

Psalm 91

Whoever dwells in the shelter of the Most High will rest in the shadow of the Almighty.
I will say of the Lord, "He is my refuge and my fortress my God, in whom I trust."
Surely he will save you from the fowler's snare and from the deadly pestilence.
He will cover you with his feathers and under his wings you will find refuge;
his faithfulness will be your shield and rampart.
You will not fear the terror of night nor the arrow that flies by day,
nor the pestilence that stalks in the darkness, nor the plague that destroys at midday.
A thousand may fall at your side, ten thousand at your right hand, but it will not come
near you.
You will only observe with your eyes and see the punishment of the wicked.
If you say, "The Lord is my refuge," and you make the Most High your dwelling,
no harm will overtake you, no disaster will come near your tent.
For he will command his angels concerning you to guard you in all your ways;
they will lift you up in their hands, so that you will not strike your foot against a stone.
You will tread on the lion and the cobra; you will trample the great lion and the serpent.
"Because he loves me," says the Lord, "I will rescue him;
I will protect him, for he acknowledges my name.
He will call on me, and I will answer him; I will be with him in trouble,
I will deliver him and honor him.
With long life I will satisfy him and show him my salvation."

Spiritual Influence Model

Most spirits of darkness find their way into your life through generational influences, wounds, and your thoughts. These powers of darkness influence your belief, thought, behavioral, personality, and relating patterns. As the Holy Spirit reveals to you the spirits of darkness that are influencing you, by the authority of Christ in the works of the cross, send them to the cross in agreement with Him. It is because of your relationship with God that you have been given the power to join with Him to send all dark spirits to the cross. With God's thoughts, you remind these thoughts from the enemy that they are destroyed; they have no power over you based on the works of Jesus at the cross.

One way to know which spirit is advancing is by the emotion you are feeling. For example, if you are feeling rejected, chances are there is a spirit of rejection present. If you are feeling intense rage, a spirit of rage may be harassing. With God's help and authority by the power of His Word, send every dark spirit to the cross in Jesus' Name.

List the spirits of darkness that are harassing you. Use these words to help you to send them to the cross – by the authority of Jesus, the works of the cross, I send _____ spirit (or any harassing spirit) to the cross in Jesus' Name by the blood of the Lamb.

List the thoughts, feelings, and behaviors that come from the dark spirits. Write down how staying under their influence will effect your personality, relationships, and destiny.

Here is an example. The spirit of rejection:
Thoughts: I don't matter. My life has no purpose.
Feelings: Rejected, empty, lonely
Behaviors: Sleep too much, eat too little or too much, isolate self
Effect on personality: too sensitive, moody, withdrawn
Effect on relationships: stuff feelings, closed off, distant
Effect on destiny: lack any desire to achieve goals and dreams

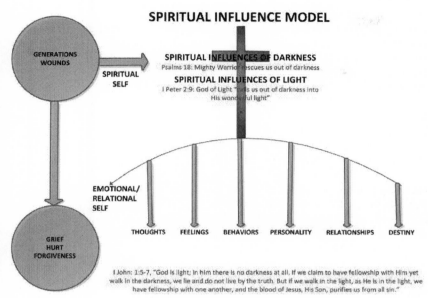

SPIRITUAL INFLUENCE MODEL

GENERATIONS
WOUNDS

SPIRITUAL
SELF

SPIRITUAL INFLUENCES OF DARKNESS
Psalms 18: Mighty Warrior rescues us out of darkness

SPIRITUAL INFLUENCES OF LIGHT
I Peter 2:9: God of Light "calls us out of darkness into His wonderful light"

EMOTIONAL/
RELATIONAL
SELF

GRIEF
HURT
FORGIVENESS

THOUGHTS   FEELINGS   BEHAVIORS   PERSONALITY   RELATIONSHIPS   DESTINY

I John: 1:5-7, "God is light; in him there is no darkness at all. If we claim to have fellowship with Him yet walk in the darkness, we lie and do not live by the truth. But if we walk in the light, as He is in the light, we have fellowship with one another, and the blood of Jesus, His Son, purifies us from all sin."

Live as children of Light
Ephesians 4:17-5: 1-21

Roselene Coblentz, Ph.D., LMFT

Your Daily Habit of Spiritual Influences of Darkness

Develop a daily habit of spiritual influences of darkness. From your sit place, worship and praise God, sending out your 911 call as needed, recognizing the advances and influences of darkness and sending them to the cross in Jesus Name by the blood of the Lamb.

Personal Growth Questions

1. What has been your past or maybe even your present view of Satan and his powers of darkness over your thoughts?

2. What challenges you to stop in your difficult situation and worship God in His nature and character as well as praise Him for what He has done for you in the past?

3. What 911 call do you need to send to Mighty Warrior?

4. What challenges you to believe God would war for you as described in Psalm 18?

5. How would your life be different if you created a daily habit of recognizing the presence of darkness in your thoughts? What challenges you to believe that God fights for you and desires to rescue you in your daily situations? Share one of your life examples when God fought for you and rescued you.

Prayer

I praise You, for You are my Rock, Refuge, Strength, and my Mighty Warrior. You fight for me. I praise You and worship You. There is no one like You. You declare war on the enemy on my behalf. You take great delight in rescuing me. You call me out of darkness because of Your covenant and eternal love for me. You call me up to war with You. I choose to join Your ranks, trusting You to strengthen me and know the way to take. I choose obedience as You speak it to me, for in my obedience it defies the enemy. With Your authority and as You help me see the advances of darkness, I remind them that their influence cannot withstand the blood of the Lamb, and I send them to the cross in Jesus' Name. I choose to take captive of every thought. May my every thought be in agreement with Your thoughts. I stand firm, believing and obeying You as You deliver me from all my fears. Mark me with deliverance, You are My Deliverer. In Jesus Name, Amen. (Psalm 18:1-18; Exodus 14:14; 2 Corinthians 10:5; Psalm 34:4)

Resources

Waking the Dead, John Eldrege
Love and War, John and Stasi Eledrege (marriage)
Possessing the Gates of the Enemy, Cindy Jacobs
Fasting, Jentezen Franklin
Shaping History by Prayer and Fasting, Derek Prince
Secrets of a Prayer Warrior, Derek Prince
Fresh Wind, Fresh Fire, Jim Cymbala
Restoring the Christian Soul, Leanne Payne
The Fight of Every Believer, Terry Law

Notes...

Week Nine: Your Journey IN the Light

In Week Eight, we focused on the enemy who desires to rule over you and your thoughts. You recognized that God will fight for you to rescue you. I hope you now understand the importance of your role and response to worship Him, call Him, and have a strategy to come out from under the enemy's influence through your authority in Christ.

As you position yourself in your "sit place with God," may you prepare in Week Nine to step into the influence of God's Light. It is here you can experience true and lasting freedom. As Paul writes: *Now the Lord is the Spirit, and where the Spirit of the Lord is, there is freedom. And we all, who with unveiled faces contemplate the Lord's glory, are being transformed into his image with ever-increasing glory, which comes from the Lord, who is the Spirit (2 Corinthians 3:17, 18, NIV).*

It is wisdom to understand how the forces of darkness undermine the forces of Light as you journey towards freedom. Believing the lies of the dark spirits is the primary strategy Satan uses to pull you into darkness. Truth always guides you to the light. With this knowledge, you must remember: God is the Light Who is always greater than the powers of darkness. You should not underestimate their influence, but remember Light always rules over darkness.

Light is associated in Scripture with redemption, love, truth, grace, and mercy—everything associated with the goodness of God. It is God's desire for you to come out from under the influence of darkness and step into the influence of His wonderful Light, as described in 1 Peter 2:9: *But you are a chosen generation, a royal priesthood, a holy nation, His own special people, that you may proclaim the praises of Him who called you out of darkness into His marvelous light (NKJV).* John also reminds us that God is Light: *He is the Light; in him there is no darkness at all (I John 1:5).* In His Light, you will experience healing, help, and the hope that you desperately need to live fully free, restored from past hurts and restored in all your relationships. *It is for freedom that Christ has set us free. Stand firm, then, and do not let yourselves be burdened again by a yoke of slavery [your thoughts in agreement with the lies of Satan] (Galatians 5:1, NIV).*

Your Role as a Child of Light

It is time for you to consider your role and response as "children of Light." As you learned in Week Four from "Your Grace Place," you are loved, valued, accepted, healed and forgiven. By choosing to live a holy, righteous, and pleasing life, you defy the enemy and all the forces of darkness. In response to the work God has done for you, by the works of Christ displayed at the cross, you come into agreement with God. Therefore, as a follower of Christ, you have been given authority by the cross of Christ to send spirits of darkness to the cross in Jesus' Name. There they are defeated and destroyed.

Paul speaks to this: *The weapons we fight with are not the weapons of the world. On the contrary, they have divine power to demolish strongholds. We demolish arguments and every pretension that sets itself up against the knowledge of God, and we take captive every thought to make it obedient to Christ (2 Corinthians 10:4, 5, NIV).* As the Holy Spirit of Truth reveals to your spirit the spirits of darkness that are influencing your life, you not only send them to the cross, but you invite the Spirit of Light to come where darkness has resided. For God has declared, *You are a chosen people, a royal priesthood, a holy nation, God's special possession, that you may declare the praises of him who called you out of darkness into his wonderful light (1 Peter 2:9, NIV).*

Then remain in agreement with the words of God to Saul on the Damascus road, *I am sending you to them to open their eyes and turn them from darkness to light, and from the power of Satan to God, so that they may receive forgiveness of sins and a place among those who are sanctified by faith in me (Acts 26:17-18, NIV).* Using the authority Christ has given you to take captive every thought positions you to enjoy the life God has designed you for.

● ● ●

This is your stance in your Grace position: you are *God's chosen people, holy and dearly loved... (Colossians 3:12, NIV).* You must have nothing to do with any lie that comes against this truth, as declared by God to you. When the enemy comes with the lies: you are not loveable or you are unworthy or you are a failure, you can exchange that lie for truth based on the words and works of Christ. This is God's Grace which you must fully wrap your heart and mind around. It is a finished work that you must make good on in how you live your life. You live centered in His love and grace to you from your "sit place with Abba God." All your life challenges get worked through from this loved center position - relationship.

This is your Truth position, as Paul declares to you: *God is light; in him there is no darkness at all. If we claim to have fellowship with him and yet walk in the darkness, we lie and do not live out the truth. But if we walk in the light, as he is in the light, we have fellowship with one another, and the blood of Jesus, his Son, purifies us from all sin (1 John 1:5-7, NIV).* You either choose to believe the lie or the truth. As children of Light, by believing truth you are able to live out the truth in your beliefs, thoughts, behaviors, and relationships, which renders the enemy powerless. Paul encourages you in 2 Corinthians 10:5 to take every thought "captive" to make it agree with Christ. You must come into agreement and choose to no longer think and live as the world does, which is separated from the grace and truth of God in Christ Jesus.

This is your stance: live as children of Light. You are a child of Light, *living out goodness, righteousness, truth, and we do what pleases the Lord (Ephesians 5:9, 10, NIV).* Put selfishness to the cross in Jesus' Name by the blood of the Lamb, and come under the influence of selflessness as Christ's example, choosing to be mindful of others, showing kindness and care for them. Always ask yourself, "What would love have me do?"

Vince's Story

Vince, from his sit place, remembering the view from the lodge widow overlooking the majestic mountains of Colorado, pours out his heart to God. "God, it is time for me to take a stance against the enemy's lies and trust You. I trust that You love me, and from this loved place, I choose to no longer believe alcohol is greater than Your power. I choose to believe I can say no and say yes as appropriate. I no longer believe I am weak, but I am strong because Christ is in me. I choose to develop healthy relationships and

• • •

financially make better decisions. I choose You and others to help me. No more secretive behaviors. I let You and others into those places I have been afraid to address. I will remain in Your loving presence to receive all the help I need."

As a child of Light, come into agreement with Paul's words, *Get rid of all bitterness, rage and anger, brawling and slander, along with every form of malice. Be kind and compassionate to one another, forgiving each other, just as in Christ God forgave you (Ephesians 4:31, 32, NIV)*. This passage vividly expresses coming out from the realm of darkness into the realm of Light and the behaviors that follow. Thus your life will reflect the character of God in the fruit of His Spirit. *But the fruit of the Spirit is love, joy, peace, forbearance (patience), kindness, goodness, faithfulness, gentleness and self-control (Galatians 5:22, 23, NIV)*.

As a child of light, you create a lifestyle that forgives, shows kindness, acceptance, compassion, and does not allow anger in any of its forms to rule in your thoughts, behaviors, or relationships. This does not mean you don't set healthy boundaries. Healthy boundary setting is needed for healing and strong, connected relationships. Developing character as you understand the "fruit of the Spirit" is a daily endeavor, utilizing every opportunity to grow and mature. Choosing faithfulness to God, self, and others is vital to defy darkness and embrace the light. Remember you are on a journey growing within your relationship with God.

Let Love Define You

As a child of Light, let love define you! You cannot love apart from God's love, which has been *poured out into our hearts through the Holy Spirit, who has been given to us (Romans 5:5, NIV)*. It is only as God pours His love into your heart that you can love as Children of Light. *Love is patient, love is kind. It does not envy, it does not boast, it is not proud. It does not dishonor others, it is not self-seeking, it is not easily angered, it keeps no record of wrongs. Love does not delight in evil but rejoices with the truth. It always protects, always trusts, always hopes, always perseveres. Love never fails (1 Corinthians 13:4-8, NIV)*.

And once again from your Grace position: "As God's chosen people, holy and dearly loved," we choose to *clothe ourselves with compassion, kindness, humility, gentleness and patience. Bear with each other and forgive one another if any of you has a* grievance against someone. *Forgive as the Lord forgave you. And over all these virtues put on love, which binds them all together in perfect unity (Colossians 3:12-14, NIV).* Take the love journey from your loved place, being deeply loved by God.

You can do this! From your Grace stance: *But by the grace of God I am what I am (I Corinthians 15:10 NIV).* And from your Truth stance: *I can do all this through him who gives me strength (Philippians 4:13 NIV). For it is God who works in you to will and to act in order to fulfill his good purpose (Philippians 2:13 NIV).*

Children of the Light
By Hillsong

Children in the wilderness
Following the love You poured out for us
Covered by the Name that we confess
Jesus Saviour forever

Roaming through the dark of night
Clinging to the word that burns deep inside
Eyes fixed on Your Name and endless light

Jesus Saviour forever
Set alight to follow
In the shadow of Your Name
The world is Yours and I know
Everything will find its place
Under Your Name

Walking on through the fire
Knowing I will not be burned but refined
Fearless in Your Name ever by my side
Jesus Saviour forever

Taking on the raging storm
Anchored to the kingdom unshakable
Holding to Your Name that outshines all
Jesus Saviour forever

Running through the wild
Dancing in the fire
Taking back what the devil had stolen

Calling on Your Name
Breaking every chain
Jesus everlasting freedom

Retrieved from http://www.azlyrics.com/lyrics/hillsonglive/childrenofthelight.html

Spiritual Influence Model

As you step into the Light you will begin to change your thinking/believing/behavorial/ relating patterns to match the Spirit of Light. For example, after coming out from rejection and under the influence of God's acceptance and self-acceptance, your thoughts/behaviors would look like this: *I am loved and accepted. My life matters. My life has meaning and purpose.* Your behaviors would then be positive and constructive, serving you well in your relationships and destiny. Then, by your spirit hear God call you out of darkness, out from under its influence and step into the Light as God is the Light. For example, in your "sit place with Abba God," hear Him call you out from the darkness of Rejection and call you in to the light of Acceptance. Here are a few more examples: Fear for Perfect Love; Anxiety for Peace; Lies for Truth; Anger for Harmony; Depression for Contentment; Judgment for Mercy; or Pride for Humility.

SPIRITUAL INFLUENCE MODEL

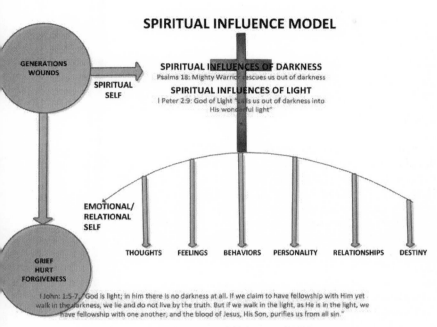

SPIRITUAL INFLUENCES OF DARKNESS
Psalms 18: Mighty Warrior rescues us out of darkness

SPIRITUAL INFLUENCES OF LIGHT
I Peter 2:9: God of Light "calls us out of darkness into His wonderful light"

GENERATIONS
WOUNDS

SPIRITUAL
SELF

EMOTIONAL/
RELATIONAL
SELF

THOUGHTS   FEELINGS   BEHAVIORS   PERSONALITY   RELATIONSHIPS   DESTINY

GRIEF
HURT
FORGIVENESS

I John: 1:5-7, "God is light; in him there is no darkness at all. If we claim to have fellowship with Him yet walk in the darkness, we lie and do not live by the truth. But if we walk in the light, as He is in the light, we have fellowship with one another, and the blood of Jesus, His Son, purifies us from all sin."

Live as children of Light
Ephesians 4:17-5: 1-21

Roselene Coblentz, Ph.D, LMFT

Your Daily Habit of Spiritual Influence of Light

Develop a daily habit of spiritual influence of Light. From your sit place, step into The Light: living loved, saved, forgiven, healed, valued, and holy, purified lives.

One Final Note

As God does His healing work in your life, He desires you to join the ranks of the Mighty Warrior's army, where He trains you up and sends you out to declare His rule and glorious reign. He desires you to join Him in the work of the kingdom, using the gifts He has given you. God is looking for those who are willing, within their circumstances, to be trained up as warriors. Will you give Him permission? Hopefully you will say YES to warrior training!

What this means is you will say yes to praising and worshiping Him in all your circumstances. Yes to committing yourself to dialogue with Him from your sit place. Yes to telling yourself the truth, and embracing His Grace, as well as making good on the help of His grace to walk out what He speaks to your heart.

A warrior in training will also choose with God's grace to forgive, allow God to heal every hurt, and welcome the God of Comfort to sit with you in your grief. In your training, you will stand firm and strong to take captive every thought that the enemy sends your way. You will send it back to the sender by the way of the cross. A strong warrior will choose to walk daily in the Light; living loved, saved, forgiven, healed, valued, and holy lives.

Remember that your training camp is your present difficult situation: for example: as a teacher in your classroom, in your marriage, your work place, with your boss or co-worker, your three-year-old, in your finances, in searching for a new job, in your singleness, or in your relational loss. It is in this place, Mighty Warrior desires to train you up. You will learn in Week 10 and Week 11 that He will also train you with the help of six companions and teach you how, in humility, to serve others. I trust you will embrace all that God wants to train and equip you to be: strong, steady, and secure in Christ as His warrior.

The last half of Psalm 18 lays out the-Mighty Warrior's training and triumph:

As for God, his way is perfect: The Lord's word is flawless; he shields all who take refuge in him. For who is God besides the Lord? And who is the Rock except our God? It is God who arms me with strength and keeps my way secure. He makes my feet like the feet of a deer; he causes me to stand on the heights. He trains my hands for battle; my arms can bend a bow of bronze. You make your saving help my shield, and your right hand sustains me; your help has made me great. You provide a broad path for my feet, so that my ankles do not give way. I pursued my enemies and overtook them; I did not turn back till they were destroyed. I crushed them so that they could not rise; they fell beneath my feet. You armed me with strength for battle; you humbled my adversaries before me. You made my enemies turn their backs in flight, and I destroyed my foes. They cried for help, but there was no one to save them— to the Lord, but he did not answer. They all lose heart; they come trembling from their strongholds. The Lord lives! Praise be to my Rock! Exalted be God my Savior! He is the God who avenges me, who subdues nations under me, who saves me from my enemies. You exalted me above my foes; from a violent man you rescued me. Therefore I will praise you, Lord, among the nations; I will sing the praises of your name (Psalm 18:30-41, 45-49, NIV).

Melody's Story

Stepping into the realm of Light, Melody welcomes the spirit of worthiness. "I step into the spirit of worthiness as Jesus has secured for me by the works of the cross." She chooses to come into agreement with thoughts of worthiness: "I am loved, valued, fully accepted, and my life has purpose and meaning because of what Christ has done for me." As she takes her early morning walk, believing God walks alongside her, she commits to hold on to these truths. Melody realizes it will take time for these truths to root deeply in her beliefs, but in the meanwhile she will choose to be kind, accepting, and loving to herself. She will tell herself the truth when the lies try to ensnare her again. She will be more committed to spend time with her friends who have repeatedly desired to spend time with her. Melody prays, "Abba God, as my friends desire to spend time with me, I choose to believe you love me and you too desire to spend time with me. May my daily walks always welcome You. I want to feel loved, accepted, valued, and enjoyed with You and my friends." It is Melody's desire to daily choose openness and acceptance in her intimacy journey with God and her friends.

Personal Growth Questions

1. Ask God to put His finger on one area of your life, or one thought pattern you believe is influenced by darkness.

2. How has that darkness affected your view of yourself, others, God?

3. What Light of truth do you need to step into to counter that darkness? Over the course of this week, meditate on that truth and speak it to yourself. Write down at the end of the week what influence this light has had on the darkness.

4. What challenges you most to stay in the Light of truth, not returning to the influence of darkness? What can you do going forward to walk in that light?

5. How would your life look differently if daily you chose to walk in God's truth and grace as a child of Light?

Prayer

God, Your word says, "Where the Spirit of the Lord is, there is freedom." I desire Your freedom over my life. Where there is my freedom, my transformation; there is Your glory, Your ever-increasing glory! I desire for my life to reflect Your grace, goodness, and glory. Open my eyes to see the darkness of my own lies and the ways the enemy deceives me. Remove my blinders. I choose to embrace truth, as You are Truth. It is Your blood that cleanses and purifies me and makes it possible for me to walk in the light as You are the Light. You have called me into Your marvelous, magnificent, and wonderful light. My heart is grateful. It is a work I could never do. It is under the influence of Your Light I want to live my life. In Your light, I choose to live as a child of light. Purify and make me holy as You are holy. Mark my life with kindness, compassion, forgiveness, acceptance of others, patience, humility, joy, self-control, gentleness, holy, pure, and selflessness as You pour your love into me by the Holy Spirit. For You are Holy and You are my Light. You are my Freedom. In Jesus Name, Amen. (2 Corinthians 3 :17-18; I Peter 2:9; Acts 26:17,18; I John 1:5-7; Ephesians 4:31, 32; I Corinthians 13:4-8; Galatians 5:22, 23; Colossians 3:12-17; Romans 5:5)

Resources

Waking the Dead, John Eldredge
Love and War, John and Stasi Eledredge (marriage)
Possessing the Gates of the Enemy, Cindy Jacobs
Fasting, Jentezen Franklin
Shaping History by Prayer and Fasting, Derek Prince
Secrets of a Prayer Warrior, Derek Prince
Fresh Wind, Fresh Fire, Jim Cymbala
Restoring the Christian Soul, Leanne Payne

Week Ten:
Your Everyday, Personal Growth Journey

Welcome to Week Ten. This week I want to provide you with a concept of growth-focus versus goal-focus and introduce you to six valuable friends to come alongside you on your everyday life journey.

Growth Focus vs. Goal Focus

Life is a journey, a daily process towards change, growth, and betterment. Results are not the only or primary aim. I want to present a broader perspective to you of growth-focus. We live in a culture that focuses almost exclusively on goals and results. Achieving a goal does give results which at times are needed. But if setting and achieving goals is the only way you proceed with your life, you will often get discouraged and quit. Goals have their purpose within the growth-focus, but your eyes must be focused on the growth, not the goals.

Goals usually have an expiration date on them, and though your goal may have been met, there is often a greater need for further growth. Therefore, your pursuit of growth is the greater purpose. To focus on the goal, the step in front of you alone, does not create sufficient energy to sustain you on your life-long journey. Goal-focus gives you a more narrow view, whereas growth-focus widens your perspective, gives you greater purpose, and a deeper, ongoing, commitment for your growth and betterment.

Some Examples of Growth Focus

Here are a few examples of what I mean by growth-focus. In marriage, you may choose for your growth-focus to develop a strong marital connection. Some of your specific goals or steps to journey towards that growth-focus might be to daily express love-communicating behaviors (whatever you decide those are), setting aside a weekly date time, intentionally listening to each other face-to-face, validating each other's feelings, affirming strengths and behaviors, or solving problems together. The primary focus remains on a strong marital connection, not the steps themselves to achieve it. Or perhaps your growth-focus is improving your physical well-being. Therefore, your steps may be more exercise, better nutrition, good sleep, or stress management. If intimacy with God is your growth-focus, then you may choose to be intentional in developing your "sit place with God," studying the Word of God, or you may commit to praying for others, forgiving others, taking time to worship God, or sharing life in community.

Over the last 30 years, I have discovered eight valuable companions needed to successfully journey with an emphasis on growth-focus—to finish the race and complete the tasks you and I have in the kingdom of God. I have already discussed two—truth and grace—and now I want to share with you six others: perseverance, tenacity, resilience, perspective, support, and endurance. Here is how I define them.

Perseverance.

Pressing forward, pushing through the challenge is the essence of perseverance. Perseverance is often needed when you want to break a habit or you are desiring something greater for your life or family. *And not only that, but we also glory in tribulations, knowing that tribulation produces perseverance; and perseverance, character; and character, hope (Romans 5:3-4 NKJV).* To have a healthy marriage and family, for example, you may have to push through saying no to drinking and yes to shared times with family. Many families are broken and separated due to alcoholism or other addictions.

Tenacity.

To never give up, to hold firmly to the truth, and to stay on task will demand the strong companion of tenacity. *Therefore, my beloved brethren, be steadfast, immovable, always abounding in the work of the Lord, knowing that your labor is not in vain in the Lord* (I *Corinthians 15:58 NKJV*). Many relationships are unhealthy due to a lack of boundaries. It is important to never give up when a healthy boundary can offer good in a relationship, even though it would be easier to give up or give in. For example, if you are a person who allows others to take advantage of you or get involved in your world without your permission, it is important to communicate your thoughts with them face to face. Share with them what they can and cannot do. Tell them friendship is important to you, but you want them to ask you versus assuming. Keep communicating your yes's and no's. It will produce healthier relationships with those who value relationship with you.

Resilience.

When the forces of life knock you down, resilience is needed to stand tall and strong beside you, to help you up, to complete the God-given task before you. *However, I consider my life worth nothing to me; my only aim is to finish the race and complete the task the Lord Jesus has given me—the task of testifying to the good news of God's grace (Acts 20:24, NIV).* For example, if you are pursuing financial freedom and you feel knocked down when your car needs major repairs beyond your budget, get back up and challenge yourself to work with your monies and trust God to provide what you don't have.

Support.

Life was not meant for us to journey alone. Support is another powerful companion. God reminds you He is with you always and will never leave you on your own. He also encourages you to support one another, to come alongside each other in your joys and struggles. *Therefore, as God's chosen people, holy and dearly loved, clothe yourselves with compassion, kindness, humility, gentleness and patience. Let the message of Christ dwell among you richly as you teach and admonish one another with all wisdom through psalms, hymns, and songs from the Spirit, singing to God with gratitude in your hearts (Colossians 3:12, 16, NIV).* For example, a husband whose wife has died needs the support of other men to spend time with him in social settings, to pray for him, and check in on him regarding his daily needs during this time of transition. Another example is a single woman desiring marriage. There is much value in married women spending time with her to encourage and pray for her as well as enjoying social times of games, movies, or dinner together.

Perspective.

The role of perspective is two-fold. It is essential to see your present situation as one part, one step, or one season of your life story. And secondly, it is important to see your present challenge from God's viewpoint, from the beginning of your life to its end. *And we know that in all things God works for the good of those who love him, who have been called according to his purpose (Romans 8:28, NIV).* For example, many women who are in a "waiting for marriage" stage of their journey have to keep focus on their present season of growth as God speaks it to them as well as being reminded that their life does move from season to season. This season is not their entire life.

Endurance.

And lastly, and definitely not the least of the eight, is endurance. It is defined as going the distance for as long as it takes to fully and completely experience growth in one part of your journey in order to be prepared for the next step of your journey. Visualize this as a door opening to a long passageway that, if traveled well, opens to another door to another life passageway. Each contributes to specific growth, but linked together, they build on each other. God works all your experiences in the mix of your past, present, and future to grow and develop you. As you journey well, *not perfectly*, but in agreement with Him, you are able to encourage others to travel alongside you as you pursue being an example to others. *Those who trust in the Lord are like Mount Zion, which cannot be shaken but endures forever (Psalm 125:1, NIV).*

Adam's Story

Adam has worked out with a personal trainer for the last three years. This discipline has helped to deeply ingrain in him the truth that meeting specific goals and results is always second to the greater overall picture of growth. As CEO of his company, "leadership by example" was the primary growth-focus of his physical workout. He desired to display to his organization "well being" by his choices, with the hope of inspiring them to improve their lives in the ways that they could. Along with his commitment to working out, he offered financial workshops, communication resources, and nutritional vending machines as well as incentives to volunteer in the community. He was a regular at Habit for Humanity, giving of his time on Saturdays.

Vice President Jay shared, "There are few men out there like Adam. He lives his life in the way that he can encourage others to do the same. He doesn't tell others to do something he is not willing to do himself. If he meets someone that is struggling with his or her health, he invites that person to go to the gym with him. If he is aware of a financial need or medical challenge, he will meet them for lunch and find a way to serve them."

Adam knows that daily he must invite perseverance and perspective on his life journey. Time is his greatest challenge, his tension point, and he has to commit to what is most important in how he spends his time. His first commitment is to his alone time with God, next time shared with his wife and family as well as his workout times, and then his business and all his employees that he desires to serve. It is no easy task to manage his time, but from his sit place, he and God manage his time commitments. To please God and honor Him is Adam's greatest desire. From this flows his influence for God's kingdom.

Remember from Weeks Eight and Nine what you learned about the role of your thoughts in the influences of both darkness and light. To journey well towards change and growth, your thoughts matter. What you choose to entertain and believe will determine your direction. Choose well and they will serve you well. I pray you journey well, believing truthfully and taking the steps needed to fulfill your desires for growth in any area of your choosing.

● ● ●

Growth-Focus Model

First, create your own growth-focus, such as developing a strong marital connection, choosing a healthy lifestyle, or becoming a mentoring leader. Second, list the goals that will help you navigate towards your growth-focus. If marital connection is your growth focus, the list might look like this: connect daily with your spouse with special messages, arrange a date weekly, read a book together, volunteer monthly together, check in with each other emotionally, plan a getaway weekend, or create a dream night. Third, list the emotions desired when you reach the fulfillment of each goal and continue to journey towards your greater growth purpose. Emotions that may result in fulfilled goals to enjoy a strong marital connection would be feeling loved, secure, connected, peaceful, encouraged, or supported. Steps for becoming a mentoring leader might include developing communication skills, praying for your group, taking personal time to keep growing yourself, meeting with your group individually, and caring for their needs.

As you move forward with your goals to growth, do not exit when you stumble or fail to fulfill one of the steps. Remind yourself that your usual exits only lead to false comfort and compromise. As you begin your journey make a commitment at every tension point to push through, press forward, and not give up. If you fall, get back up; keep your God-view in front. Run to your finish line that you might testify to the glory and grace of God.

Remember to pursue the greater value of your growth and betterment, knowing that each goal pursued along the way will follow, with the desired emotions. To develop any area, break a habit, or stronghold, ask yourself—what is the greater growth I desire? For example, if you want to stop smoking, the growth focus would possibly be a healthy lifestyle, or if you want to get out of debt, it could be financial freedom. This journey of growth-focus requires trusting God with your whole heart that He will go before you as Isaiah describes: *I will go before you and will level the mountains; I will break down gates of bronze and cut through bars of iron. I will give you hidden treasures, riches stored in secret places, so that you may know that I am the Lord, the God of Israel, who summons you by name (Isaiah 45:2, 3, NIV).* Take hold of the mindset: Never give up, for God never gives up on you. You will succeed if you hold to the truths and pattern your daily habits on Joshua 1:5-9 and Acts 20:24.

* * *

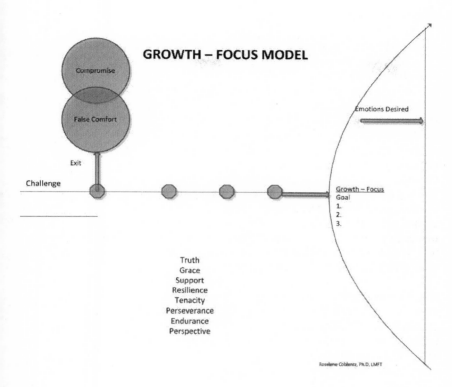

GROWTH – FOCUS MODEL

Compromise

False Comfort

Exit

Challenge

Emotions Desired

Growth – Focus
Goal
1.
2.
3.

Truth
Grace
Support
Resilience
Tenacity
Perseverance
Endurance
Perspective

Roselene Coblentz, Ph.D, LMFT

Your Daily Habit of Growth-Focus

Develop a daily habit of growth-focus. From your sit place, create your steps that will move you forward to enjoying the fulfilling of your growth desire and enjoy the emotions with each successful step. Welcome your eight companions to journey with you.

Personal Growth Questions

1. What is one growth-focus you would like to begin? List the steps you believe are needed to move you in that direction.

2. Of the six friends, describe how one of them in particular has helped you on your life journey. Describe the particular circumstance(s) in which this companion helped you.

3. Of the six friends, which one do you feel is most needed in your life right now? What do you need to do to integrate it consciously on your growth-focus journey?

4. This week focus on one of these friends and intentionally invite it into your present circumstances. At the end of the week, write down how focusing on this companion has helped you.

5. What influence do you desire your life to have? On what individuals? What steps might you take to exercise that influence?

Prayer

God, You are Faithful and Good. You will always love me. You are Perfect Love to me. I remind myself that it is Your great love and compassion that is my ever strength in difficult times. Your mercy comes to me fresh every morning. Great is Your faithfulness to me, to help me to persevere, to push through and endure, going the distance in all my difficulties. From my sit place, I patiently, expectantly wait on You. You will work in me, both to will and do for Your good pleasure. As I choose to journey with You, You will work all things out for my good and the fulfilling of Your good purposes in me. I hold on to this perspective. I choose to never give up or quit. I will hold tight to resilience and tenacity, utilizing their strength. I trust You will take this journey with me. This is our journey together. You will never leave me alone or on my own. You are my support and help. It is Your purpose in my challenges to make me strong, develop character and bring me to maturity in Christlikeness. You make me strong when I am weak as I trust You with my whole heart. I pray that as I journey with you, You will mark my life with perseverance, resilience, tenacity, resilience, and perspective as You are Strong and the God of my life. In Jesus Name, Amen. (I John 4:19; Lamentations 3:21-23; Philippians 2:13; Romans 8:28; James 2:2, 3; I Corinthians 9:12 NIV)

* * *

Resources

Developing the Leader Within You, John Maxwell
Maxwell 3-in-1 Special Edition: Winning Attitude/ Developing the Leaders Around You/Becoming a Person of Influence, John Maxwell
Make Today Count: The Secret of Your Success is Determined by Your Daily Agenda, John Maxwell
The Maxwell Daily Reader: 365 Days of Insight to Develop the Leader within You and Influence Those Around You, John Maxwell
Spiritual Leadership: Moving People onto God's Agenda, Henry Blackaby
Spiritual Leadership:A Commitment to Excellence for Every Believer, J. Oswald Sanders
Courageous Leadership, Bill Hybels

Notes...

Week 11: Your Spiritual Core

Welcome to Week 11. I trust that the last ten weeks have been edifying and encouraging to you in your intimacy journey with God. I pray that you will commit to practicing these as a daily lifestyle as you move forward on your journey.

I hope that you are developing more consistently your intimacy with God, inviting Him in on all of your life circumstances. Where you need to be truthful, you choose to tell yourself the truth; where you need to accept the grace of God, you receive the fullness of His love by His death for you; where you need to forgive, you forgive; where you need healing, you invite the Presence of Jesus to heal your heart; and where you need to grieve, you welcome the God of Comfort to sit with you. I hope that you have a greater understanding of the spiritual forces of darkness and recognize the enemy's advances in your life, agreeing with the works of Christ, sending them to the cross in Jesus' Name by the blood of the Lamb. I trust you are choosing to "live as children of Light," bringing joy and delight to God's heart and pursuing a life journey of change and growth.

Here in Week 11, I want to invite you to consider your influence from four core values. At the very center of your being are identity, intimacy, and integrity, which then flow out to your fourth core value, humility. You have the most influence when you develop these three at your core and then, like a waterfall, release them to flow in loving others, from a servant's heart, with humility. It is imperative that you develop a strong core so that you can stand, no matter the storm that may enter your world. Your personality, roles, position, ministry, or finances do not belong in your core because they do not have sufficient sustaining power to deal with a major crisis. Your relationship with God from these three values will provide for you the strength, hope, and help you will need, no matter your challenge.

Identity. First, your identity is in Christ. This means that your relationship, your position with God, is not based on your works or performance. Your identity as His beloved son or daughter is not based on what you do or don't do; it is based on what He did for you. You need only to believe and receive His grace. There is no greater identity that will sustain you in all of your life circumstances.

Your identity consists of God's truthful words to you about His relationship to you as your God and Creator. The words that were spoken to Daniel by God are true for you too: *'Don't be afraid,' he said, 'for you are very precious to God. Peace! Be encouraged! Be strong!' (Daniel 10:19, NLT).* If your parents failed to share with you how much you are loved and valued, how beautiful and strong you are, all that is special about you as a person, it is imperative that you take God at His word and believe Him. These are His personal words to you: you are *God's chosen people, holy and dearly loved (Colossians 3:12, NIV).*

If needed, return to Week Four on Grace, and spend time in your sit place to take into your heart God's deep love and desire for relationship with you. His desire for you has nothing to do with your performance. Believe every word He has to say to you about your value and acceptance, because this is the basis of your identity in Him. You are who God says you are. You are not what your wounds speak to you from past experiences, your personal judgments about yourself, what unhealthy relationships may have conveyed to you, nor what the media portrays to you. You are what God says you are!

This is your identity: holy and dearly loved. Your identity has been secured by God. It is from this identity that you develop your intimacy, your personal relationship with God. Hold fast to this Scripture: *Once you had no identity as a people; now you are God's people. Once you received no mercy; now you have received God's mercy (1 Peter 2:10, NLT).*

Chase's Story

Here is how Chase embraces his secured identity in God. Chase told his dad,

"While hiking in the mountains of Colorado, "I was struggling with the loss of my marriage. The trail had steep drop offs, and I had to walk carefully to safely reach my destination. But fear seemed be traveling with me, trying to convince me that the loss of my marriage was going to send me over the edge, and I would never recover." Chase continued, "But it was like I heard God's voice, the Holy Spirit, saying to me, 'You are My son, My very much loved son. You belong to Me. I am here to help you. Do not fear; trust Me. You can trust Me to show you the way. I have a plan for your future, and it is good. You are My son, and I will restore your soul.'"

Intimacy. Intimacy is developed from your personal "sit place with God," your daily, ongoing dialogue with Him. Just as in human relationships, you cannot develop intimacy in human relationships without a deep sharing of your thoughts and feelings, so is it true with God. As you experience life, you share with Him your struggles, worries, fears, challenges, hurts, joys, and desires, trusting His love to care for you and work out all things for your good because you love Him and He loves you. You share with Him your thoughts, your feelings about those thoughts, and your deep desires and longings within each and every daily life experience. Then you choose to listen to His voice through the Holy Spirit, His truthful words reminding you of your secured identity in Him, and trusting what He shares with you in response to what you have shared with Him.

Communication is the dialogue that keeps you connected, no matter your situation. This connection opens up the way for your obedient response. Your obedience is a very powerful dimension of developing intimacy with God. It is similar to your human relationships: when someone shares with you what you can do to care for his heart, you follow through. Refer back to Week One to practice this core value. God values your response in loving Him through your obedience.

Here is one definition of intimacy that may help you along this intimacy journey with God and then with others. Intimacy is the daily awakening in your relationship(s) that leads towards openness, vulnerability, nurturing acceptance, being fully enriched and satisfied in closeness, and a deepening desire and delight to know and be known within the relationship. There is no end to growing intimacy; it is a daily pursuit for a lifetime. Start your intimacy journey with God and then allow it to flow to other trustworthy relationships.

Psalm 34 exemplifies this intimacy: *I will bless the LORD at all times; His praise shall continually be in my mouth. My soul shall make its boast in the LORD; The humble shall hear of it and be glad. Oh, magnify the LORD with me, And let us exalt His name together. I sought the LORD, and He heard me, And delivered me from all my fears. They looked to Him and were radiant, And their faces were not ashamed. This poor man cried out, and the LORD heard him, And saved him out of all his troubles. The angel of the LORD encamps all around those who fear Him, And delivers them. Oh, taste and see that the LORD is good; Blessed is the man who trusts in Him! (Psalms 34:1-8, NKJV).*

Bob and Abigail's Story

Look at how both Bob and Abigail develop their intimacy with God in their daily experiences. Bob stops at his favorite coffee shop early every morning before going to the office where he practices law. He journals his prayers to God and then listens to His voice by the Holy Spirit. He values the truth that God hears him, but he is most encouraged that God speaks to him. This time provides a peace that allows him to be centered before he enters into the demands and pressures of his day. He takes time to read the Word, to know God's voice. The last 15 minutes of his time, Bob continues reading "Humility," by Andrew Murray. This time prepares him as he meets with his men's group every Monday night to encourage and support each other. After her early morning run, Abigail sits with her cup of tea in her favorite red chair to spend some time with God. She listens to Sons and Daughters' "Oh How I Need You," meditating on the words as her prayer to God. She writes in her journal the encouraging words she hears the Lord share with her. Psalm 119 is her focus for this month to continue to know God's voice. She ends her time praying for her husband, using Stormie Omartian's books, "The Power of a Praying Wife Devotional" and "The Power of a Praying Wife, Book of Prayers." She values her prayer group where she can be vulnerable and encouraged and then support and pray for others.

Integrity. It is from your identity in Christ and your intimacy with Him that you will discover the pathway towards a lifestyle of integrity. This is the third dimension of developing a strong spiritual core. Pursuit of God is your highest calling and the basis of your integrity. Perfection is not the goal. You are only as strong as you believe truthfully and receive gracefully all that God speaks to your heart. This is why your personal relationship with God must be nurtured daily. Only in this relationship will He shape and form you into Christ-likeness. From this place of personal intimacy with God, you listen, trust, and obey the words He speaks to you. Obedience is imperative;

only full obedience, not partial, is acceptable to God.

Your integrity is revealed in your life by your attitude, character, choices, and responses as displayed in the fruits of the Spirit: *But the fruit of the Spirit is love, joy, peace, longsuffering, kindness, goodness, faithfulness, And those who are Christ's have crucified the flesh with its passions and desires. If we live in the Spirit, let us also walk in the Spirit. Let us not become conceited, provoking one another, envying one another (Galatians 5:22, 24-26, NKJV).*

Your integrity is also revealed in living as children of light as you studied in Week Nine. Your words and behaviors need to match. How you live your life privately needs to be the same publicly. Practice daily these words from the Scriptures: *...And walk in love, as Christ also has loved us and given Himself for us...Walk as children of light (for the fruit of the Spirit is in all goodness, righteousness, and truth),...be filled with the Spirit, speaking to one another in psalms and hymns and spiritual songs, singing and making melody in your heart to the Lord, giving thanks always for all things to God the Father in the name of our Lord Jesus Christ, submitting to one another in the fear of God (Ephesians 5:2, 8-9, 18-21, NKJV).*

Kathleen's Story

Kathleen shares with her friend Jan, "Over the past 20 years I have been developing these core values of identity, intimacy, and integrity. Day by day, I have tried to use every challenge as an opportunity to invite God in, sharing my heart and listening to His. Then I have tried to walk out what He speaks."

This has been reflected in her healing journey of her childhood. Kathleen's dad died when she was five. Her mom struggled with alcohol therefore Kathleen often had to care for herself. She had to do her homework by herself as well as figure out what to eat. By the age of 12, she went to live with her grandparents, her dad's parents. Her life began to improve with love and nurture from them. But Kathleen did not see her mom often and deeply missed both of her parents. She had to learn to practice forgiveness and to allow God to heal her heart in the ways she was hurt by her mom's choices. God comforted her in her deep losses of childhood. Kathleen valued the words He shared with her. His words provided the love, grace, truth, and hope she needed to depend on daily. Now she has committed herself to practice Christlikeness at every opportunity. She continues to share with her friend, "It is not about perfection, because I sometimes fall short, but it is about my consistent progressing toward being all God created me to be and do."

Daily she meets with God, believing He loves her and will help her with every problem and concern. Kathleen says, "I want to experience His love every day, no matter my situation, and express my love to Him in loving others. Just as Jesus obeyed God, my heart desire is to trust and obey the One who loves me with His heart and life. *If you keep my commands, you will remain in my love, just as I have kept my Father's commands and remain in his love. My command is this: Love each other as I have loved you (John 15:10, 12, NIV).* As Kathleen continues to live her life from her core values, every week she keeps her commitment to her elderly neighbor to pick up groceries for her, even though her life sometimes feels overwhelming, working full-time as an accountant and caring for her four children as a single mom. But God's love for her and her love for Him flows through her to loving her children and others.

Humility. Humility is the fourth value that is needed to strengthen your core. It is the outflow of your identity, intimacy, and integrity in your relationship with God. Humility is the bending low to lift up another, the same heart of Christ expressed in Philippians 2: *Who, being in very nature God, did not consider equality with God something to be used to his own advantage; rather, he made himself nothing by taking the very nature of a servant, being made in human likeness. And being found in appearance as a man, he humbled himself by becoming obedient to death— even death on a cross (Philippians 2:6-8, NIV).* As James reminds us, *God resists the proud, but gives grace to the humble (James 4:6, NKJV).*

Kathleen's servant heart to her neighbor reveals a commitment to serving others from a place of humility. It is not an add-on to her life, from a "should" place to get God to love her, but flows from her love back to God. She values serving humbly in caring for a friend's need. Matthew says it so well: *Yet it shall not be so among you; but whoever desires to become great among you, let him be your servant. And whoever desires to be first among you, let him be your slave— just as the Son of Man did not come to be served, but to serve, and to give His life a ransom for many (Matthew 20:26-28, NKJV).*

Humility is your heart attitude in serving others. Here are a few more examples: medical teams serve in places where they give of their time and assets to those who could never repay them. It is also shown when a family of five will care for another family of five children so their parents can have some time away. Or when monies saved for a family vacation are given away due to another's need for moving expenses and much needed car repairs. Serving others from the place of humility puts value on him or her. There is no greater gift of humility to offer to another than to honor them as God-created individuals in sharing in their needs.

As you continue daily to strengthen your spiritual core, humility will be the overflow of your personal relationship with God. Be very mindful that it is the outflow, separate from your identity. It is an honor to serve and love others. It is important to learn to bless others' giftedness and accomplishments, focusing on their growth and betterment, versus undermining them with negativity and fault-finding. The enemy will do that very well without your help. You do not want to be in agreement with the enemy, but in agreement with God, choosing to forgive, pray, serve, love, and help one another on life's journey. Together, you can each lead by example, learning and growing from each other. *Then Jesus said to his disciples, "Whoever wants to be my disciple must deny themselves and take up their cross and follow me. For whoever wants to save their life will lose it, but whoever loses their life for me will find it. For the Son of Man is going to come in his Father's glory with his angels, and then he will reward each person according to what they have done (Matthew 16:24-25, 27, NIV).*

God measures people by the small dimensions of humility and not by the bigness of their achievements or the size of their capabilities.
Billy Graham

If you plan to build a house of virtues, you must first lay deep foundations of humility.
Augustine

Christ is the humility of God embodied in human nature; the Eternal Love humbling itself, clothing itself in the garb of meekness and gentleness, to win and serve and save us.
Andrew Murray

Spiritual Core Model

Your identity is sealed and secured by God through the work of the cross of Christ. Believe every word He says to you. Who you are is who He says you are. Hold tight to His word: *Once you had no identity as a people; now you are God's people. Once you received no mercy; now you have received God's mercy (1 Peter 2:10, NLT)*. Hold on to His true words in every situation, no matter how difficult it is. This makes for a strong identity.

From your sit place with God develop your intimacy. Dialogue with Him, using your journal. Daily write down your thoughts, feelings, and all that concerns you. Then pause and listen and write down what God shares with you. Trust that you can hear the Holy Spirit as His voice to you. Meditate on Psalm 34:1-8. Let His Word to you be a constant and consistent in all of your experiences.

Your integrity flows from your identity and intimacy with God. His love to you and your love to Him will guide you to develop a daily life of integrity. Be committed to ensure your words match your behaviors, both privately and publicly.

Lastly, develop humility, daily bending low to lift up another on their life journey. Remember this is what Christ did for you. *You must have the same attitude that Christ Jesus had. He humbled himself in obedience to God and died a criminal's death on a cross (Philippians 2:5, 8, NLT)*. In this attitude of humility, Christ came to serve which is his example to us as Matthew states, *Just as the Son of Man did not come to be served, but to serve (Matthew 20:28, NKJV)*.

Let the same words that Jesus spoke to the disciples help you daily develop a strong spiritual core. *As the Father loved Me, I also have loved you; abide in My love. If you keep My commandments, you will abide in My love, just as I have kept My Father's commandments and abide in His love. This is My commandment, that you love one another as I have loved you (John 15:9-10, 12, NKJV)*.

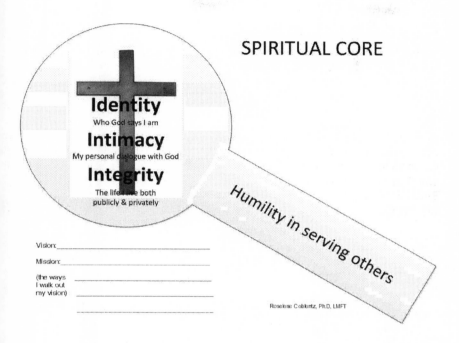

SPIRITUAL CORE

Identity
Who God says I am

Intimacy
My personal dialogue with God

Integrity
The life I live both
publicly & privately

Vision:_____

Mission:_____

(the ways
I walk out
my vision) _____

Humility in serving others

Roselene Coblentz, Ph.D, LMFT

Your Daily Habit of a Strong Core and Humility

Develop a daily habit of a strong core. From your sit place, exercise daily your spiritual core and embrace humility at the heart of your service to others. Stay true to your God-given vision and mission. Commit to a daily progression of Christlikeness in your daily habits for a lifetime.

• • •

Your Vision Statement

One last thought for you to consider in serving others. I believe God created you with a vision for your role in the kingdom of God. Within that vision is your mission: how you walk out your vision in serving others. I encourage you to write down your vision statement given to you by God: the one thought that defines you. Keep it short; perhaps a few words will capture it. Some examples are: restored relationships, worship warrior, financial carrier, or creative. Then write down your mission: the ways you walk it out daily in your life. For example, mine is restored relationships and how I walk it out is in five ways: counseling, mentoring, teaching, writing, and praying. Remember that not all will be present in all seasons of life. You gradually will learn the ways to walk out your vision as you daily, year after year, walk with God.

Permanence

To end our journey together, here is my last word: "permanence." I want to speak to this most powerful word as you continue on your God journey. Permanence is defined as "the quality or state of being permanent or lasting." In other words, what you see is who I am consistently: the only change from day to day is I get better and better over time!

A life of permanence is a consistent lifestyle of growth and betterment, nurtured by daily habits of well-being. It is important to reflect to the watching world the life of Christ in our daily responses to life experiences. It is not putting on a Sunday dress, but wearing our everyday life values both privately and publicly. What the world needs to see from morning to night is Christlikeness. What the world (your husbands, wives, children, bosses, co-workers, neighbors, and all others) sees in our daily habits must be the very essence of our being. It is how we live our lives day in and day out; what is seen in the open places is the same behind closed doors. Only then can we have influence for greater growth and betterment to the world around us.

Permanence is not an ongoing striving towards perfection. It is a daily progression of Christlikeness.

Personal Growth Questions

1. How would you characterize your identity? What words define you?

2. In what ways does your self-definition not align with God's view of you? How can you bring your self-perception into line with God's perception?

3. Of the core values outlined in this chapter, which one(s) do you find most difficult for you? What do you need to do to practice and to integrate this value in your life?

4. Describe some of the ways you sacrifice yourself to serve others.

5. What is your vision statement (the one thought that defines you) and the mission (the ways you walk out your vision in serving others)?

Prayer

God, You are Good, You are good to me. You are Perfect Love. You are loving to me. From my sit place, I desire to trust You with my whole heart; trusting in Your truthful words to me. This is my identity in You. My identity is secure in You. I choose to share my thoughts and feelings; receiving Your care and comfort for my heart and then listening to Your words of truth. I choose to take Your grace and walk them out in obedience. This is our intimacy, our shared life together. You love me and my obedience is my loving you back. Thank You for desiring intimacy, relationship with me. I want my life to reflect your grace, goodness, and glory. Therefore, I count my life worth nothing except to live it with integrity, my words matching my behaviors that are true to Your character and the life of Christ in me. I desire to complete my assigned task as You speak it to me. Make known to me my vision and the ways I am to walk it out in my mission for the kingdom of God. Most of all, as I serve others, I desire to serve with humility; bending low to lift others up just as You say, "I am gentle and humble in heart." Mark my life with a strong spiritual core of identity, intimacy, and integrity. May my life be to the praise and glory of God. Mark me with a servant's heart in gentleness and humility. For You are Truth, Grace, Love, Gentle, and Humble in heart. In Jesus Name, Amen, (Proverbs 3:4, 5; John 15:9, 10; Acts 20:24; Matthew 28:11)

Resources

Developing the Leader Within You, John Maxwell
Maxwell 3-in-1 Special Edition: Winning Attitude/ Developing the Leaders Around You/Becoming a Person of Influence, John Maxwell
Make Today Count: The Secret of Your Success is Determined by Your Daily Agenda, John Maxwell
The Maxwell Daily Reader: 365 Days of Insight to Develop the Leader Within You and Influence Those Around You, John Maxwell
Moving People onto God's Agenda, Henry Blackaby
Spiritual Leadership: A Commitment to Excellence for Every Believer, J. Oswald Sanders
Courageous Leadership, Bill Hybels
Humility, Andrew Murray
Absolute Surrender, Andrew Murray

Notes...

Week Twelve: Your Daily Habits

You have arrived at week 12. I trust you have journeyed faithfully through each week, experiencing more of His great love and grace to you. I hope you will not see this as a formula, but a daily, relational journey with you and God, and those God desires you to invite along your life journey. We have come to the end of our journey together, yet I trust it is just the beginning of a deeper intimacy journey with you and God.

I am adding one more model, putting it all together for you to use as an example of how to work this knowledge within your everyday situations. I pray you will make good on God's Grace and His Word as you develop your daily habits in all of your life experiences. Your life is about taking one step at a time, listen to the Holy Spirit of what habit needs to be invited in on your step by step journey. I hope what drives your life is your passion and purpose to know God and be known by Him. May you receive His healing grace, grow deeper in your personal relationships, and continue to serve others with the same humility of Christ.

• • •

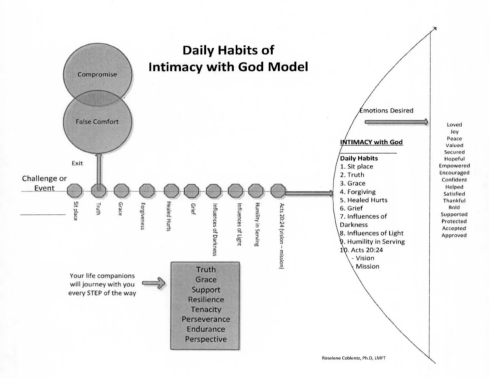

Daily Habits of Intimacy with God Model

Compromise

False Comfort

Exit

Challenge or Event

Sit place · Truth · Grace · Forgiveness · Healed Hurts · Grief · Influences of Darkness · Influences of Light · Humility in Serving · Acts 20-24 (vision – mission)

Emotions Desired

INTIMACY with God

Daily Habits
1. Sit place
2. Truth
3. Grace
4. Forgiving
5. Healed Hurts
6. Grief
7. Influences of Darkness
8. Influences of Light
9. Humility in Serving
10. Acts 20:24
    - Vision
    - Mission

Loved
Joy
Peace
Valued
Secured
Hopeful
Empowered
Encouraged
Confident
Helped
Satisfied
Thankful
Bold
Supported
Protected
Accepted
Approved

Your life companions will journey with you every STEP of the way

Truth
Grace
Support
Resilience
Tenacity
Perseverance
Endurance
Perspective

Roselene Coblentz, Ph.D, LMFT

Your Daily Habit of Intimacy
Develop a daily habit of intimacy. From your sit place, journey daily with God, step-by-step, practice your daily habits in your every day life situations.

Daily Habits to Intimacy with God Model

As you begin each day on your journey, or if working through a challenge, log it on the model. Remember your situations have a greater purpose: intimacy with God, character development, healing of relationships, and its overflow into loving and serving others. See yourself taking one step at a time to develop your daily habits of intimacy within your life experiences.

Daily Habits: Sit Place, Truth, and Dual Grace

Your daily habit of "sit place," is always your first step, your first stop. Whatever your situation is start by sharing your thoughts and feelings with God. Receive His care and comfort as you share and then listen to His voice of truth. If you are using a journal write your thoughts and your feelings first, pause, and then write what He says to you. Remember, His words to you will match the words and principles of the Word of God. Listening to His truth words for your particular situation will move you into step two, your daily habit, Truth. Hold on to His true words as you enter into step three, your daily habit of Dual Grace. Remember and receive daily His love by His sacrificial death for you, reminding your self you are deeply loved by Him. No matter your circumstances, never let go of His grace work for you. Also in step three, take His grace and walk out what He speaks to your heart to do in your present circumstances. Do not exit; listen, trust, and obey His loving, truthful words to you. He is trustworthy and has your very best in mind. These three need to be present no matter what your experience. They will be your greatest strength and help no matter the storm that may have entered into your world.

Daily Habits: Forgiveness, Healed Hurts, and Grief

As you navigate through steps four through six, embrace your daily habits of forgiveness, healed hurts, and grief. Be faithful to listen to the voice of God and check in by asking yourself: Is there someone I need to forgive, is there a hurt that needs healing, and or is there a loss I need to pause and grieve. Remember, you are working through your each and every daily situations through each step, to grow your relationship with God, bring healing to your heart, and strengthen your relationships with others.

Daily Habits: Influences of Darkness and Light

Step seven is your daily habit of recognizing with your spirit what spirits of darkness are harassing you. This is a valuable habit to develop to step out from under the influence of lying thoughts and holding firmly to truth; the truth that will set you free. And then to make a commitment to your daily habit, living as a child of Light. Choosing to love, forgive, serve with humility, show compassion and mercy, set healthy boundaries, tell yourself the truth, be kind, submit to others as to The Lord, live a holy and pure life, and love God with all your heart, soul, mind, strength.

Daily Habit: Growth-Focus and 8 Companions

As you develop your specific growth-focus, take your eight companions with you. They are your life companions and will be with you every step of the way, starting with your sit place with God.

Daily Habit: Spiritual Core and Serving Others with Humility

Step ten has two focuses. Daily make strong your spiritual core. In your identity, believe what God says is true of you. Believe only His voice, making it your own. Daily dialogue with God about everything that concerns you. He loves and cares about you. Live your life with integrity. Be committed that your words and behaviors match the life of Christ. The second focus is your daily habit of serving others in humility. Practice in each of your situations to serve others, bending low to lift them up. As you serve them, may they enjoy feeling loved, accepted, encouraged, strengthen, helped and respected by you. Lastly, remember: Acts 20:24, However, I consider my life worth nothing to me; my only aim is to finish the race and complete the task the Lord Jesus has given me—the task of testifying to the good news of God's grace (NIV). Practice this habit within the vision given to you by God and in the ways (mission) you serve others daily.

Tension Points

Remember, as you step by step move towards intimacy with God, practicing your habits, you will experience tension. The tension is to go to your sit place and meet with God or ignore the importance of it; or to tell yourself the truth or hold on to faulty thinking; to forgive or not to forgive, take the time to ask God to heal a hurt or dismiss your hurt; deny caring for your grief waves; neglect to listen to the Holy Spirit as to what spirits are harassing you and choosing to give into your fleshly desires versus living as a child of Light. Consider the tension to develop a strong core by making time for it in your schedule or filling up your day with many other seemingly more important activities. There will be the tension to be humble in serving others or engaging in pride, serving self. Do not exit when the tension increases. If you do, you will experience comfort but it is a false comfort leading to compromise. All growth comes from tension. Inviting your companions will help you to push through your tension points. Work through the tension with your relationship with God, believing truthfully you are loved and He is your strength and help.

Companions

Don't forget to take your companions on your journey. They will help you develop your daily habit in each step you take in your situation. Remember to invite The Life Companion, Jesus, to travel with you. He promises to be with you always. Take note this is not a linear journey, but one that has valleys, peaks, twists, and turns. As you journey, consider these words from Proverbs, *Trust in the LORD with all your heart, and lean not on your own understanding; In all your ways acknowledge Him, and He shall direct your paths (Proverbs 3:5-6 NKJV).*

Emotional Dimension

While you are on this intimacy journey, list the emotions you desire to experience. If you want to enjoy them you will need to commit to the journey; never give up, never quit. It is not about perfection, but progression. As you journey one step at a time you will increasingly enjoy more of these emotions that are connected to your daily habits.

Personal Growth Questions

1. Share what your experience has been within your relationships from these three words after journeying these last 11 weeks.

Trustworthy: Do I trust God and others more? Can others trust me more?

Transparency: Am I more consistently sharing my real thoughts and feelings uncensoredly with God and others? And can they share genuinely with me?

Acceptance: Do I feel more loved and accepted by others when they share truthfully to me? Do they feel more loved when I speak into their life?

2. Share one event or situation that you have processed through, step by step with your daily habits.

Last note from Roselene

It is always challenging to say good-bye to those you love when your life moves you to another city, church, or your season of friendship changes. I am grateful to have journeyed with you as the author. As we part ways, I pray that you will forever hold true to your intimacy journey with God within all of your life experiences. May "Daily Habits of Intimacy with God" serve as a conduit to help deepen your relationship with Him and be a reminder as to how to process all of your life challenges. It is for freedom that Christ has set you free! May you receive grace blessings on your intimacy journey with God, enjoying redeemed-restored relationships, and serving others for the kingdom of God!

Roselene

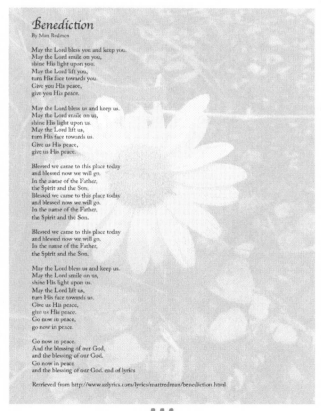

Benediction
By Matt Redman

May the Lord bless you and keep you.
May the Lord smile on you,
shine His light upon you.
May the Lord lift you,
turn His face towards you.
Give you His peace,
give you His peace.

May the Lord bless us and keep us.
May the Lord smile on us,
shine His light upon us.
May the Lord lift us,
turn His face towards us.
Give us His peace,
give us His peace.

Blessed we came to this place today
and blessed now we will go.
In the name of the Father,
the Spirit and the Son.
Blessed we came to this place today
and blessed now we will go.
In the name of the Father,
the Spirit and the Son.

Blessed we came to this place today
and blessed now we will go.
In the name of the Father,
the Spirit and the Son.

May the Lord bless us and keep us.
May the Lord smile on us,
shine His light upon us.
May the Lord lift us,
turn His face towards us.
Give us His peace,
give us His peace.
Go now in peace,
go now in peace.

Go now in peace.
And the blessing of our God,
and the blessing of our God.
Go now in peace
and the blessing of our God. end of lyrics

Retrieved from http://www.azlyrics.com/lyrics/mattredman/benediction.html

"Amazing Grace (My Chains Are Gone)"
Chris Tomlin

Amazing grace
How sweet the sound
That saved a wretch like me
I once was lost, but now I'm found
Was blind, but now I see

'Twas grace that taught my heart to fear
And grace my fears relieved
How precious did that grace appear
The hour I first believed

My chains are gone
I've been set free
My God, my Savior has ransomed me
And like a flood His mercy reigns
Unending love, amazing grace

The Lord has promised good to me
His word my hope secures
He will my shield and portion be
As long as life endures

My chains are gone
I've been set free
My God, my Savior has ransomed me
And like a flood His mercy reigns
Unending love, amazing grace

The earth shall soon dissolve like snow
The sun forbear to shine
But God, Who called me here below,
Will be forever mine.
Will be forever mine.
You are forever mine.

Retrieved from azlgrics.com

* * *

Your Daily Habits of Intimacy with God

Your Daily Habit of Prayer

Develop a daily habit of prayer. Prayer is relationship, built in your "sit place with God." You dialogue with Him personally; then listening, trusting, and obeying the words He speaks to you. You live internally/eternally first, and then that response flows externally to those with whom you have influence.

Your Daily Habit of Truth

Develop a daily habit of truth. From your sit place, assess your everyday thoughts, replacing faulty self-talk to match God's thoughts. Believing truthfully is displayed powerfully in what you *do* personally and relationally.

Your Daily Habit of Dual Grace

Develop the daily habit of "dual" Grace. From your sit place, trust the God of all Grace to do for you what you cannot do for yourself, and making good on the grace of God to do what is yours to do as He speaks it to you.

Your Daily Habit of Forgiveness

Develop a daily habit of forgiveness. From your sit place, forgive others and yourself with the grace of God and live daily in the truth, "I am forgiven."

Your Daily Habit of Healed Hurts

Develop a daily habit of healed hurts. From your sit place, share your hurts with God, listening and receiving His comfort and compassion and healing words of truth. He will teach you a new way of remembering your story, a Jesus story.

Your Daily Habit of Grief

Develop a daily habit of grief. From your sit place, grieve well your losses. The God of Comfort will care for your sadness. As you continue your grief journey make a place for joy to sit beside sadness.

* * *

Your Daily Habit of Spiritual Influences of Darkness

Develop a daily habit of spiritual influences of darkness. From your sit place, worship and praise God, sending out your 911 call as needed, recognizing the advances and influences of darkness and sending them to the cross in Jesus Name by the blood of the Lamb.

Your Daily Habit of Spiritual Influence of Light

Develop a daily habit of spiritual influence of Light. From your sit place, step into The Light: living loved, saved, forgiven, healed, valued, and holy, purified lives.

Your Daily Habit of Growth-Focus

Develop a daily habit of growth-focus. From your sit place, create your steps that will move you forward to enjoying the fulfilling of your growth desire and enjoy the emotions with each successful step. Welcome your eight companions to journey with you.

Your Daily Habit of a Strong Core and Humility

Develop a daily habit of a strong core. From your sit place, exercise daily your spiritual core and embrace humility at the heart of your service to others. Stay true to your God-given vision and mission. Commit to a daily progression of Christlikeness in your daily habits for a lifetime.

Your Daily Habit of Intimacy

Develop a daily habit of intimacy. From your sit place, journey daily with God, step-by-step, practice your daily habits in your every day life situations

Who I Am In Christ

Biblical Truths to "Practice Believing"

I AM GOD'S...

- possession Gen 17:8/1Cor 6:20
- child John 1:12
- workmanship Eph 2:10
- friend James 2:23
- temple 1 Cor 3:16/6:16
- vessel 2 Tim 2:2
- co-laborer 1 Tim 5:18
- witness Acts 1:8
- soldier 2 Timothy 2:3
- ambassador 2 Cor 5:20
- building 1 Cor 3:9
- husbandry 1 Cor 3:9
- minister/instrument Acts 26:16/1 Tim 4:6
- chosen Eph 1:4
- beloved Rom 1:7/2 Thess 2:13
- precious jewel Malachi 3:17
- heritage 1 Pet 5:3

I HAVE BEEN...

- redeemed by the blood Rev 5:9
- set free from sin /condemnation Rom 8:1-2
- set free from Satan's control Col 1:13
- set free from Satan's kingdom Eph 2
- chosen before foundation of world Eph 1:4
- predestined to be like Jesus Eph 1:11
- forgiven of all my trespasses Col 2:13
- washed in the blood of the Lamb Rev 1:5
- given a sound mind 2 Tim 1:7
- given the Holy Spirit 2 Cor 1:22
- adopted into God's family Rom 8:15
- justified freely by his grace Rom 3:24
- given all things pertaining to life 2 Pet 1:3
- given great and precious promises 2 Pet 1:4
- given ministry of reconciliation 2 Cor 1:22

- authority over the power of enemy Luke 10:19
- access to God Eph 3:12
- been given wisdom Eph 1:8

I AM...

- complete in him Col 2:10
- free forever from sin's power Rom 6:14
- sanctified 1 Cor 6:11
- meet for the Master's use 2 Tim 2:21
- loved eternally 1 Pet 1:5 /
- eternally kept in the palm of his hand John 10:29
- kept from falling Jude 1:24
- kept by the power of God 1 Pet 1:5
- not condemned Rom 8:1-2
- one with the Lord 1 Cor 6:17
- on my way to heaven John 14:6
- quickened by his mighty power Eph 2:1
- seated in heavenly places Eph 1:3
- the head and not the tail Deut 28:13
- light in the darkness Matt 5:14
- candle in a dark place Matt 5:15
- city set on a hill Matt 5:14
- salt of the earth Matt 5:13
- his sheep Ps 23 / Psalms 100:3/ John 10:14
- a citizen of heaven 1 Pet 2:11
- hidden with Christ in God Psalms 32:7
- protected from the evil one 1 John 5:18
- kept by the power of God 1 Pet 1:5
- secure in Christ John 10:28-29
- set on a Rock Psalms 40:2
- more-than-a-conqueror Rom 8:37
- born again 1 Pet 1:23
- a victor 1 John 5:4
- healed by his strips Is 53:6
- covered by blood of Jesus Rev 12:11, 1 Pet 1:19
- sheltered under his wing Psalms 91:4
- hidden in secret place of the Almighty Ps 91:1

I HAVE...

- access to the Father Rom 5:2
- a home in heaven waiting for me John 14:1-2 • all things in Christ 2 Cor 5:17
- a living hope 1 Pet 1:3
- an anchor to my soul Heb 6:19
- a hope that is sure and steadfast Heb 6:19
- authority to tread on serpents Luke 10:19
- power to witness Acts 1:8
- the tongue of the learned Isaiah 50:4
- the mind of Christ 1 Cor 2:16
- boldness and access Heb 10:19
- peace with God Rom 5:1
- faith as a grain of mustard seed Luke 17:6

I CAN...

- do all things through Christ Philp 4:13
- find mercy and grace to help Heb 4:16
- come boldly to the throne of grace Heb 4:16
- quench all the firey darts Eph 6:16
- tread on the serpent Luke 10:19
- declare liberty to captives Isaiah 61:1
- pray always and everywhere Luke 21:36
- chase a thousand Joshua 23:10
- defeat (overcome) the enemy Rev 12:11
- tread Satan under foot Rom 16:20

I CANNOT...

- be separated from God's love Rom 8:35-39
- be perish or be lost John 10:28, John 3:16
- be moved Psalms 16:8
- be taken out of my Father's hand John 10:29
- be charged or accused Rom 8:33
- be condemned 1 Cor 11:32

● ● ●

Reference

Author, Richard W. LaFountain
http://www.prayertoday.org/2004/PDF/Guides/Who-I-Am.PDF

Notes...

Notes for Small Group Facilitators

Prayer (You may pray this prayer out loud before each week's session.)

God, we give thanks to You and worship Your most holy name, O Most High. We declare Your loving kindness in the morning and Your faithfulness every night. God, as we meet together, I pray that You come and sit with us. Share Your truth with us. The truth that will set us free. May we take Your truth and allow it to shape us and form us into Christlikeness. May we each hear Your voice, the Holy Spirit, in the ways we need to hear Your truth. May we come humbly to listen, trust, and obey what You speak to us personally. May the Real Presence of Jesus minster grace and peace to each one present. May the blood of Jesus and the work of the cross hold back every strategy and plan of the enemy. All glory and honor be given to you. It is You we need. We are utterly dependent on You. Work in us to will and do for Your good pleasure. Come. We welcome You. In Jesus Name Amen.

Helps for Each Week

You may begin with an ice breaker. (A list is provided if you desire.)

Pray over your group the prayer above or one of your own as God leads you.

Together, each week work through the teaching, model, and discussion questions. Encourage each to share, but be gracious to those that are new to sharing in a group setting. Be encouraging, but not forceful, showing acceptance and grace to each on their journey.

During each week, be faithful to pray for each person in your group based on the things they share. Daily keep bringing them to Jesus to do His grace work in their lives. Encourage members in the group to connect with each other for support and encouragement.

A prayer is presented to close each week's session. It is available for those who are not comfortable in saying their own prayers. I encourage facilitators who are willing to pray this out loud or use their own prayer at the end of each week's discussion.

You may desire to close with a worship song. One idea: Benediction, Matt Redman

Here is my prayer for you as leaders.

God, I pray for every leader who chooses to facilitate a group to take this Intimacy journey. Weekly, show yourself strong and loving to them. Deliver to them each week truth-grace in all the ways they need You. May they hear Your voice, the Holy Spirit, as they prepare each week and lead their group to know You and all that You have for them. Protect them by the blood of Jesus and the way of the cross from every strategy and plan of the enemy. Open the way for them to taste and see: You are good, You are faithful, You are loving, and You are powerful. May they experience Your Real Presence in Jesus daily. Pour out Your Spirit on them. Grace them with Your peace and help every week. Bless their Intimacy journey as they develop their daily habits in knowing You. In Jesus Name, Amen.

Tips for Effective Small Group Facilitators

(True Stories Ministries)

Develop a sense of individual and group trust.

It's good to remember that most people have ambivalent feelings about being in small groups. They are unsure if they'll fit in, if they have anything worth contributing, if they will be treated with respect and dignity, and if they are genuinely liked and appreciated by other group members. If those issues aren't recognized and addressed early on, members can dry up and blow away without ever giving a hint they were in trouble. People need to feel that they are a valuable part of the group. And while it is important for each person to make an effort to communicate value to the others, the leader can go a long way in setting the pace for that kind of appreciation and respect.

Have an attitude of servanthood.

Take advantage of opportunities to praise the group members' strengths, talents, and abilities in front of the others.

Maintain positive eye contact and good non-verbal communication.

Use humor appropriately.

Remember two simple rules: (1) Be yourself to help effectively communicate key concepts to your group, not simply entertain them. (2) Avoid using others' weaknesses or slips (like mispronunciations) to humor the group.

Model good listening skills.

Many times, people say one thing but mean something totally different. Good listening skills not only hear what is said verbally, but listen to "why" something was said or "what" was truly meant by the spoken words.

* * *

Use the Salt principle.

Salt makes people thirsty, and the goal of this principle is to create a thirst for constructive conversation in which both you and your group can learn about each other's needs. Simply, it means to never communicate information you consider to be important without first creating a burning curiosity within the listener. For example, "This next concept is one of the most important things that I've learned. It has done more for me as a missionary than anything else." This type of statement forces others to thirst for the next concept you are referring to.

Use good discussion questions.

A good question is one in which members discover truth for themselves. Therefore, don't ask questions that have one correct answer (e.g., "Is training important?"). Furthermore, there are several different kinds of questions, each designed to elicit different information. Some of those types are:

Information and opinion: What do you think?

Relational: How do you feel?

Experiential: What was that like for you?

Self-disclosure: What is a fear you have?

In order to ask good questions, we encourage you to think about some of these rules:

Practice good listening skills.

Ask questions to draw out someone's discussion.

Encourage questions but stay focused on the theme.

Postpone questions that don't apply to the session.

Promote application to the principles. "How are things going with this area?"

Promote transparency by being transparent as a leader.

Promote the safety of trust and support.

The group must support confidentiality about personal areas.

Be personal and caring. People respond to genuine caring.

Encourage honesty but discourage a harsh spirit.

Truth can be overwhelming if it is not shared in a genuine loving spirit.

Look for ways to encourage each participant in their own personal growth.

Be transparent.

This can be a fearful thing for any leader, but the payoff is well worth it. As one veteran of small groups has put it, "What I lost in impressiveness, I gained double in approachability."

Share your appropriate failures and struggles.

Maintain a respect for and sensitivity to each group member.

Regardless of his or her background or faults, each person is valuable and has a unique

contribution to make to the group.

Keep the group on schedule.

There's a real art to this, because every group gets off track some time and there's nothing wrong with that. Though time is limited for your small group sessions, if you control things too rigidly, your group can become frustrated in thinking that they're not being allowed to express themselves.

Keep discussions on the central subject while still allowing room for some digression.

Some guidelines to follow are:

Prevent more talkative members of the group from rambling; don't be afraid to interrupt and carry on.

Permit those who are not as talkative more latitude in getting off the subject. What you lose in temporary continuity you gain in their long-term input and involvement.

Diffuse argumentation. If an argument or disagreement starts, don't allow it to continue. If you can reconcile the problem quickly, do so. Otherwise, defer it until after the session is over and meet with the parties involved.

Use questions to guide them back, such as, "That's an interesting point, Jim.

Let's get back, though, to what we were saying a moment ago."

Additional questions for initiating deeper, meaningful conversation
(from "Sticky Jesus" by Toni Birdsong and Tami Heim)

⇒ How did that happen?

⇒ How can I pray for you?

⇒ How can I help you?

⇒ How did that make you feel?

⇒ How are you really doing today?

⇒ What do you plan to do next?

⇒ What scares you the most about that?

⇒ What's the worst that can happen?

⇒ What do you need right now?

⇒ What else do you want to share?

⇒ Why do you feel that way?

⇒ Why does that matter to you?

⇒ Why are you so down today?

⇒ Why don't you tell me more?

More neutral: (online through Global Business Woman Forum)

⇒ What have you been thinking about lately?

⇒ What's been on your mind?

⇒ What are you excited about at the moment?

⇒ When was the last time you made a difference to somebody?

⇒ Who are you really happy for at the moment?

⇒ When was the last time you felt inspired?

⇒ If you could be in your dream place at the moment what would you be doing?

⇒ If somebody was describing your personality what would they say?

⇒ What are you most proud of?

⇒ What's been tempting you lately?

⇒ What's been the one most consistent thing in your life?

⇒ What are you sure of?

⇒ Who have you inspired lately?

⇒ What do you love about people? Or What do you love about (person's name)?

⇒ What gives you butterflies in your tummy?

⇒ When do you find time to reflect? What do you usually reflect about?

Community building questions: (from Relevant Community Church, Elkhorn, Neb.)

⇒ How did you experience, hear from or recognize God in your life this week?

⇒ Is the overall rhythm of your life moving toward God or away from God? Tell me about it.

⇒ As you pray about your life recently, what are some areas where you sense God was there but you turned away?

⇒ How are you enjoying prayer and time in the Word?

⇒ How have you been prioritizing your family?

⇒ How have you served, shared a meal with, or encouraged someone within this week?

⇒ Where do you need to offer forgiveness or ask for it?

⇒ How have you been inviting Jesus into your friendships and times together with people?

⇒ How have you been relating — or not relating — the way Jesus relates to you, with people where you live, work and play?

⇒ Who have you been intentionally talking to about Jesus Christ?

⇒ How have you been praying for or serving the community lately? How have you been sacrificially giving of yourself to God, His will and His Kingdom?

Icebreakers

Week One: Introduction to Your Intimacy Journey
Share what you hope to gain from this 12-week journey.

Week Two: Your Sit Place with Abba God
Where is your favorite place to reflect on your relationship with God?

Week Three: Your Truth Life-Preserver
Share two truths about yourself that the group may not know about you and one that is not-true.
Let the group choose which one is not-true.

Week Four: Your Grace Place
Share one experience that someone offered kindness to you when you did not expect it.

Week Five: Your Gift of Forgiveness
Share a time when you experience forgiveness.

Week Six: Your Healing Plan
What are your favorite "band-aids" when you have been disappointed?

Week Seven: Your Grief Journey
What have you done for someone who has experienced a loss or having a difficult time?

Week Eight: Your Journey OUT of Darkness
Share a time when you were afraid or felt very alone?

Week Nine: Your Journey IN the Light
Share a time when you specifically obeyed God that brought you out of darkness into the light.

Week Ten: Your Everyday, Personal Journey
Share one area you have or are presently working on to make stronger in your life.

Week Eleven: Your Spiritual Core
Share one way you have served in your church, neighborhood, or community.

Week Twelve: Your Daily Steps
Share one word that you would use to describe what God has been saying to you in the last eleven weeks.

"As the Father has loved me, so have I loved you. Now remain in my love. If you obey my commands, you will remain in my love, just as I have obeyed my Father's commands and remain in his love. I have told you this so that my joy may be in you and that your joy may be complete. My command is this: Love each other as I have loved you. Greater love has no one than this, that he lay down his life for his friends."

John Chapter 15:9-13, New International Version